QUICKBOOKS ONLINE FOR BEGINNERS 2026

The Complete User Guide To Learn And Master Bookkeeping, Inventory Management And Accounting For Businesses and Organizations Using QuickBooks With New Features And Useful Tips And Tricks

Eric Adams

Table of Contents

Introduction

QuickBooks is an accounting software company whose products include desktop, internet, and cloud-based accounting solutions for processing bills and business payments. It is primarily aimed at small and medium-sized enterprises. QuickBooks is popular among these users because of its ease of use and reporting capabilities.

QuickBooks also includes support services and features like pre-authorising electronic payments and monitoring employee time. Intuit also offers a cloud option called QuickBooks Online, which allows users to access the program through a secure login by paying a monthly fee.

The software is often regarded as simple to use and comprehend, even by company owners and users with no financial or accounting knowledge. Another advantage of QuickBooks is the readily available templates for creating graphs, company plans, invoices, and spreadsheets. It may also save time and effort for business owners by automating their signatures on business checks (which are scanned and uploaded for usage).

Chapter 1:

QuickBooks Online: All You Have To Know

How Does Quickbooks Work?

Utilizing the latest reporting technology, QuickBooks Online offers the capability of handling your bookkeeping through an affordable subscription service. However, Intuit has an on-site application for larger, more established companies, but that's not what this guide is about.

For 30-days, QuickBooks Online allows you to try out its service without risk or credit card. So, if you haven't signed up for your trial, now may be a good time.

You see, understanding how QuickBooks works requires that you dive into the software's features. Let's look at ways small businesses use QuickBooks Online for their accounting purposes.

Small Business Use Cases

With all the inundated tasks small business owners face, it's no wonder some fail to manage their organization's finances. Bookkeeping has been around for millennia, but it has never been as easy as it is these days. We live in a time of technological revolution, and it would be silly not to take advantage of it.

The benefits QuickBooks Online offers small to medium-sized company proprietors go beyond expectations for such a simple program. Enjoy the ease of use and incredible features of this intuitive application.

Create, Track, And Automate Invoices

Every company should have an invoicing system to handle daily requests, quotes, and sales. QuickBooks Online lets you create invoices, automate the payment tracking process, and place all this data into an overview of the business's receivable accounts.

You can print or email your client's invoice directly from the platform to further streamline customer communications. Once you use QuickBooks Online for your company's accounting, there may never be anything else that takes its place.

Monitor Bills And Expenses

Connecting the QuickBooks Online platform to your credit card or bank is the first step to automation. The information the software receives between the interlinked services allows it to categorize expenses automatically.

You can even manage upcoming bills with the platform's account payable option. Paying business fees, charges, or costs will never be the same again.

Generating Financial Reports

QuickBooks Online lets you stay ahead in business with its intuitive money flow and reporting tools. You can monitor three of the most significant financial reports of any company:

1. Profit and loss
2. Balance sheet
3. Statement of cash flows

Observe Employees' Working Hours And Expenses

QuickBooks Online is more than an invoicing software; it provides advanced employee expense management. You can set your staff up with an account where they can submit their claims for approval.

Once you have confirmed or denied the transaction, you can see the matching costs involved.

Payroll

Managing payroll is often a treacherous task that debilitates small business owners at the end of the month. With QuickBooks Online, these fallacies are a thing of the past!

The platform has an integrated payroll system, including access to HR, health benefits, and additional amenities offered to employers. QuickBooks Online's software offers automatic tax filing and same-day direct deposits and is supported by a tax penalty protection plan.

Track Supplies

Whether it's cleaning detergent for your washing business or rare collectible figurines you're selling, QuickBooks Online and Advanced have unique inventory tracking features.

Easily and quickly locate product lots or find individual items using the serial number inquiry system.

Streamline The Tax Process

The tax period is undoubtedly the most stressful time of the year for business owners, and rightfully so. However, QuickBooks Online records detailed data throughout the year, so you aren't left scrambling for financial statements when tax season arrives.

Your trusted accountant can log in and retrieve financial data from your QuickBooks Online account, or the statement can be printed.

Accepting Online Payments

Automated clearing houses (ACH) or credit card payments can be paid directly from a QuickBooks Online invoice. Once online payments are turned on, your clients can pay for a product or service using either of the two available methods.

First-time deposits to your account typically occur within five business days of the payment. However, your client's remittance will reflect quickly after the account is fully set up within 48 hours.

Scanning Of Receipts

QuickBooks Scan Manager allows you to easily manage scanned documents and receipts to add them to bills, sales documents, invoices, or other transactions. A simple drag-and-drop process is utilized for uploading images to the Receipts, Transactions, or Banking tab.

If you wish to email receipts to QuickBooks, they'll show up on the platform. QuickBooks Online is all about making the lives of business owners more productive.

Keeping Tabs On Mileage

Courier or taxi services love using the QuickBooks Online mobile app to track drivers' miles. You can monitor company vehicle trips from beginning to end within a few clicks.

Quickbooks Online Advantages

Scaling your company or getting funding from a third party or bank will be challenging without accurate business records. A business's financial health is the first thing investors and lenders want to know about before putting money into it.

Things could quickly become a nightmare if your books aren't up to date or you're disorganized about filing taxes. What company does the owner want to land in trouble with the IRS? Luckily, QuickBooks Online takes care of all the hassle by making its platform user-friendly.

Intuitive User Interface

Most accounting applications come with little to no educational material, are challenging to learn, and have clunky user interfaces. The design and layout of QuickBooks Online not only make managing your cash simpler but more succinct, even if you have no experience in finance or accounting.

Integration With Third-Party Applications

QuickBooks Online has a massive list of applications and services it can connect to. Whether using a third-party tax preparation program or Microsoft Excel, QuickBooks Online makes it easy to connect.

There are over 650 business apps that the platform can integrate with, including:

- Shopify
- Adobe Commerce
- Amazon Marketplace
- Google Cloud Storage Buckets
- Cleo Jetsonic
- Oracle E-Business Suite
- Microsoft Dynamics

- Acumatica
- Netsuite
- Salesforce
- SAP

Customization

Creating business plans, charts, spreadsheets, and invoices has never been easier. QuickBooks Online offers you a selection of practical templates, which can be customized to suit the business's requirements.

The customization options help make documents look professional and stand out from the competition. Company owners can add their logo, detailed sales information, or notes to inform employees or clients about something special.

Check Signing

The check signing process becomes efficient when you have the option of uploading your signature. That is useful for people who sign many checks because it saves precious time and frees availability. If you sign hundreds of checks each month, you'll love this!

Affordable Pricing

Most new companies have limited budgets to work with in the beginning stages of operation. Furthermore, if those proprietors spend an exuberant amount on accounting software, they'll be out of business in no time.

There's no need to hire an accountant to take care of your books externally, as it all happens in a single location. You can have more time and avoid paying an external vendor to maintain your transactional records.

If you have trouble learning QuickBooks Online, there's always an option to use the live bookkeeping service. A certified bookkeeper will determine your business's financial health and manage your books.

With a starting price of only $12.50 per month, QuickBooks Online is not only affordable but has robust features too. The money saved by utilizing QuickBooks Online can be put into other areas of your business.

Used By Millions Worldwide

It is one of the best accounting software programs globally, and truthfully so. Many finance firms, accountants, and bookkeepers love using this software to manage business finances.

If you have never used accounting software before or are feeling lost in the system, a qualified individual can help you. Ensure you work with someone with QuickBooks Online Certification for peace of mind.

Cloud Storage

Cloud Storage provides you access to your financial records no matter where you are. If your accountant is in the United States and you're in Australia, adding a bookkeeper to the subscription is simple.

Give these individuals access to your company file by providing them with the password and login details. Choose from a dynamic range of financial or accounting firms and get your books done correctly.

Your information is stored on Intuit's highly secure server, meaning all data remains intact if your computer malfunctions or is damaged.

Money Management

Small to medium-sized organizations love utilizing QuickBooks Pro Online for their fund handling functions. One of the top attributes of the application allows business owners to set transaction details and due dates for all recurring invoices.

You can email, print, or message directly from the application; all data is recorded for easy accessibility.

Let's not forget that the platform can connect to your bank account and download transactions. This function removes the requirement for paper bank statements and allows you to view all fiscal data in QuickBooks Online's overview.

Expense Billing

All businesses have several costs and expenses that must be taken care of to operate optimally. It could be larger fees, such as purchasing new machinery for the factory, or smaller charges for dinner or gas.

Irrelevant to the expense type, QuickBooks allows you to record each one. Moreover, expenditures are documented in correlation with the project or customer, giving you the option to search for them through the dashboard.

Sales Invoicing

Generating invoices and creating receipts are required for any company. With QuickBooks Online, you can now perform the most imperative business functions with a single click or with the shortcut keys.

When the invoice is created, it can be sent electronically to clients via email or printed. Depending on the project, you can charge your customer in large batches or separately. The former is a valuable feature that allows you to charge multiple clients for the same product or service.

Signing up for QuickBooks Merchant Services should be your go-to if you want the advantage of accepting credit cards and debit card interests.

Financial Reports

There are many financial reports users of QuickBooks Online can generate. Whether weekly, monthly, or yearly, QuickBooks allows you to consolidate data into one place. Furthermore, reports can be exported to Excel and delivered to your accountant via email. Below you'll find some of the most common financial reports you can view in QuickBooks Online:

- Trial Balance
- Statement of cash flows
- Transaction list with splits
- Recurring template list
- Transaction list by date
- Reconciliation reports
- Recent transactions
- Profit and Loss
- Recent automatic transactions
- Profit and Loss Comparison
- Journal
- General ledger
- Balance sheet
- Account list
- Balance sheet comparison

These features are the tip of the iceberg in financial reporting, so make sure to utilize them to increase company effectiveness.

Job Costing

Track expenses, monitor time, and create estimates on projects you are currently busy on. This helps you determine job profitability and run detailed cost reports to locate areas of interest.

Without accurate estimations, your business may fail to land that client you have been wanting.

Customer Support

The customer support users receive from QuickBooks Online is phenomenal. No matter what package you're on, the team at Intuit is ready and willing to assist with any issues. If there is a glitch with the software or you're stuck with the accounting, speak to the QuickBooks Online support center folks.

You can contact QuickBooks Online client services via email, live chat, or phone. As long as your organization has a paid subscription, you can access the support service unlimited times.

Training And Education

You already know that QuickBooks Online is one of the most widely used accounting programs. That said, you'll find information, tutorials, and education online to help you better manage your accounting.

Resources like this book are the first steps to getting ahead with your QuickBooks Online education.

If you sign up for QuickBooks Online Enterprise, you'll receive online training tools at no cost. You'll also get free access to QuickBooks courses for one year.

Mobile Access

Mobile access to QuickBooks Online means you can manage your business on the go. Service and subscription-based businesses benefit significantly from this feature as their clients are generally based worldwide.

Download the application to your smartphone and link it to your QuickBooks Online account.

Focused On Small Businesses

QuickBooks Online loves helping small businesses take care of their accounting requirements. The application's budget-friendly prices and intuitive, user-friendly interface make it the perfect solution for anyone needing to maintain their financial records.

If the company is growing and you need more from the software, it is a matter of a few clicks, and QuickBooks Online is upgraded. Speak to a consultant if you are unsure of the package that suits your company's requirements.

Tax Compliance

With payroll reporting and tax regulations, keeping track of all business transactions can be challenging. QuickBooks Online monitors tax laws so that its clients don't have to. Thanks to the sales tracking features, QuickBooks can report business expenses and sales tax when needed. Moreover, it prevents inconsistencies or miscalculations when sending tax return documents.

Here are the advantages of automating the accounting process in preparation for tax season:

- Improve financial record accuracy.
- Reduces bookkeeping activities like calculating expenses and income.
- Automatic report generation for analytics, tax purposes, or financial statements.
- Eliminates the need to track down crucial information as everything is stored in a single location.

Additionally, the software helps you sort and categorize expenses, so all the data is available when you need it. QuickBooks Online allows you to upload receipts or documents that are automatically segmented.

More Efficient Business Processes

You can free up time for more imperative tasks when the financial management process is streamlined with an automated accounting system like QuickBooks. Tasks, such as categorizing expenses, can be automated to limit mistakes or subsequent issues in your business's accounting.

Both old and new company owners struggle with monetary management tasks because they can be arduous. State-of-the-art software like QuickBooks allows enterprise proprietors with no experience to acquiesce to federal laws and control their accounting operations.

Better Client Relationship Management

Enabling direct payments and invoicing clients gives them a more fluid experience, allowing them to pay your business quickly by utilizing one of their favorite remittance forms.

This reduces the hassles that typically arise when clients don't pay or avoid your invoices. Any business owner wants to keep the peace with their customers, and QuickBooks can help them do it. Improve your organization's cash flow management by having consistent monthly payments.

With the extra free time you'll receive using QuickBooks; you can provide superior client services that can help grow your business exponentially.

Premium Security

QuickBooks Online is cloud-based and was developed to keep your sensitive company credentials secure. A double layer of security protects all data transferred between you and Intuit's server.

The software utilizes a 128-bit SSL encryption to encode data and keep it safe. Furthermore, your information is autonomously saved in case of system failures or a broken internet connection.

Your essential data is also backed up so it can be restored should there be an error. Safety is of the utmost importance to Intuit, and QuickBooks Online is a testament to that statement.

Accurate Forecasting

Making educated predictions to grow your business is done by understanding common trends within your enterprise. Scaling growth, planning for seasonality, and keeping your organization financially solvent can only be achieved through precise forecasting.

Raw data is turned into easily digestible analytical reports that help you plan for the future. With these insights, you can make more intelligent decisions concerning your enterprise's finances, such as cutting costs, allocating resources, or adjusting staff salaries.

Increased Productivity

With QuickBooks Online's accounting automation, various duties can be handled concisely. There'll be less time spent correcting records, inserting data, and clicking through files to retrieve reports.

Moreover, the attributes that require focus, such as approving transactions, documenting costs, and analyzing cash flow, are accelerated.

Regular Updates

Intuit constantly releases updates to iron out bugs, increase security, and add additional features. Each upgrade comes with documentation that explains the fundamental changes incurred.

Whether you subscribe to the Simple Start, Essentials, Plus, or Desktop version of QuickBooks, you can rest assured that the software always operates optimally.

Quickbooks Is Expanding

By the decade's end, QuickBooks will reach over ten million users. The propensity for growth is a sure sign that the enterprise knows what's up. Customer orientation has always been at the forefront of QuickBooks' business model, and it shines through in the applications it creates.

This characteristic has made QuickBooks one of the most popular accounting programs on the market. You should have total confidence in the software that receives hundreds of daily inquiries.

Quickbooks Is Feature Rich

You already know by now that QuickBooks is loaded with features. Although it may take time to learn each aspect of the application, it'll all be worth it in the end. QuickBooks is on its way to becoming the most widely used accounting software with all these attributes.

Every business process is taken care of through the system; you only have to set it up.

Inventory Tracking

Knowing when stock is bought or sold can help you keep tabs on your business inventory. The system utilized by QuickBooks Online allows you to enter various data, including SKUs, stock codes, and other relevant information.

Succinctly track and manage any item your business uses to make money. **Please note**: Inventory tracking is only available to Plus users of QuickBooks Online.

Electronic Payments

Electronic payments make company processes simpler. Your patrons won't have to go to a financial institute to pay your invoices because of the wide range of credit cards accepted. All invoices have a link that the customer can use to pay debts immediately.

Also, transactions performed on your business account can be automatically downloaded and documented in QuickBooks Online.

Quickbooks Pricing And Options

The software-as-a-service (SaaS) subscription model is the basis of the QuickBooks enterprise. QuickBooks Online offers four primary tiers:

- Simple Start
- Essentials
- Plus
- Advance

Quickbooks Online Simple Start

The Simple Start plan is perfect if you want primary access to the QuickBooks Online service, including reporting, expense tracking, and income statements.

Starting at $12.50 a month for the initial three months and changing to $25 monthly. This package is ideal for someone wanting to test out the platform. Manage 1099 contractors, track sales tax, accept payments, and send invoices with this basic plan.

Access to the QuickBooks Online Simple Start plan is granted to one user and their small business accounting services firm.

Quickbooks Online Essentials

Starting at $25 per month for the first three months and then increasing to $50 per month afterwards is the QuickBooks Essential plan. Including everything in the Simple Start package, this option allows you to track time, manage bills, and pay suppliers.

If you have clients globally, you'll be happy to know that this tier lets you transact and invoice in multiple currencies.

Your small business accounting services firm and three users will have access to the QuickBooks Online Essential plan.

Quickbooks Online Plus

As your company starts growing, so do the financial responsibilities of its core. With the Plus plan, you begin the first three months paying only $40 and $80 for every subsequent month.

You'll get everything from the Simple Start and Essentials packages, including purchase order creation and inventory tracking capabilities. Job profitability and project progress can also be tracked through this value-for-money plan.

Five business users and their small business accounting services company have full access to the features of the Plus option.

Quickbooks Online Advanced

QuickBooks Online Advanced gives you everything from Simple Start to Essential and Plus! This package retails for $90 per month for the initial three months, then rises to $180 every 30-days.

Company owners looking for business analytics, employee expense management, better user permissions, premium support, and advanced invoicing features should look no further than this plan.

With this top-tier package, you can provide access to the platform to over 25 users and your small business accounting service firm.

Chapter 2:

Get Started with QuickBooks Online

You've decided to take the leap and use QuickBooks Online to handle your company's finances. QuickBooks Online provides the tools required to analyze, monitor, and understand your business while performing tweaks to increase productivity.

Now that you have the power of the world's preferred accounting software in your hands, it's time to set it up to match your criteria. A general recommendation while using QuickBooks Online is to keep actions verbatim with transactions occurring in real life. Bank deposits, sales records, and invoices must be included to give you a complete picture of the company's finances.

Ensure each step is recorded precisely, even if you take out a loan from the bank, pay salaries with QuickBooks Payroll, or approve a credit card payment. Everything in your business checking account should match the entries inserted into QuickBooks Online.

For easy reference, each subsequent section begins with the actionable steps required to fulfill the desired result.

Fill In Your Company Information

1. Gear Icon

2. Account and Settings

3. Company

Filling in your company information is the initial step to getting started with QuickBooks Online. Head to the gear icon, click "Account and Settings," then navigate to 'Company.'

Ensure the business details entered are accurate because this data automatically appears on your sales forms and invoices. You'll need to enter the following particulars before continuing with the setup process:

- Company Name
- Organization Address
- Email

- Website
- Phone Number

Click the "Pencil Icon" to edit this information, and click 'Save' once all credentials are entered correctly.

We all know how vital the fiscal year end is; that's why you have to set up the tax form intended to be sent in when the time comes. Establishing a company type is crucial to determining one's tax returns.

Speak to the Internal Revenue Service (IRS) or your accountant if you need help obtaining a Social Security Number (SSN) or Employer Identification Number (EIN). These identification digits are required by anyone who operates a business in most states of America and Canada.

If you don't reside in North America, check your country's requirements with your local tax regulating agency.

Setting Up A Fiscal Year

1. Gear Icon
2. Account and Settings
3. Advanced
4. Accounting

Understanding your business's fiscal year begins and ends helps QuickBooks Online automate one of the most stressful times annually. Knowing your tax schedule is crucial for any business owner, whether they own a small, medium, or large enterprise.

Navigate to "Account and Settings," click 'Advanced,' then 'Accounting.' This menu allows you to edit the following information:

- The first month of the fiscal year.
- Accounting method.
- The first month of the income tax year.
- Close the books.

To prevent fraudulent activity on your account, you can "close the books" for the fiscal year after the first 12 months of business. This attribute prevents anyone from editing or changing the company's QuickBooks data as you prepare for tax season.

Select Your Accounting Method: 'Cash Or Accrual'

1. Gear Icon
2. Account and Settings
3. Advanced
4. Accounting

Head to the 'Accounting' tab to configure the accrual or cash method for reporting business income. New companies generally utilize the cash method as it's more straightforward to track expenses and earnings. However, some benefits stem from both options.

Consult with your accountant to find out which accounting method suits your business. Once you begin with a particular accounting system, it's challenging (but not unachievable) to change to another.

Select Your Currency

1. Gear Icon
2. Account and Settings
3. Advanced
4. Currency

Under the 'Advanced' tab, you'll find 'Currency.' If you have a client who doesn't use your local currency, the multicurrency option can help you track foreign currency transactions. Your customers' home currency is the one they will pay in when they purchase products or services.

Add A Business Logo

1. Gear Icon
2. Account and Settings
3. Company Name

Without a logo, your company will fail to stand out. Customize QuickBooks Online to add professionalism to the overall customer experience. Head to "Account and Settings," and click "Company Name."

Here you can place a logo or visual representation of your brand that'll appear on all your sales receipts, estimates, and invoices sent to clients. Below is advice on how to upload a vibrant logo effectively:

1. Use a file size of less than 1MB.
2. Choose a square logo for superior rendering.
3. Only utilize .gif, .bmp, .jpeg, .jpe, or .png file formats.
4. Use a 24-bit color depth or less with the standard RGB color space.
5. Ensure the image has a white or transparent background to merge with the invoice uniformly.

Adjusting Default Terms For "Net Payment"

1. Gear Icon
2. Account and Settings
3. Sales
4. Sales Form Content

The client must know the payment date if you're about to send your first invoice. The "Account and Settings" menu is where you can change your default payment invoice terms and make general adjustments.

Select "**Due on receipt**" from the dropdown menu if you want payment immediately. Otherwise, choose a satisfactory period or create personalized payment criteria through the **+Add New** function.

The default terms are locked once this process is completed. However, terms for separate invoices are edited directly on the form.

How To Set Up Sales Tax

1. Left Menu
2. Tax Tab

Most states require business owners to collect sales tax if they sell products. Once your account is established, click the "Tax Tab" and navigate to the setup module. Here you'll be asked for information regarding where you sell your products and for how much. Before proceeding, ensure the cash or accrual accounting method is selected (speak to an accountant if you need advice.)

Finding out how much you owe is done through the Sales Tax Liability Report, available in the top right-hand corner. Sales taxes can also be attached to your invoices, making it simple to store them coherently.

Do You Require Inventory Tracking?

1. Gear Icon
2. Account and Settings
3. Sales

Planning for the future is vital to an organization's success. If you plan to manage your inventory or stock levels, now is a great time to turn on the Track feature.

Choosing to start tracking from the beginning is excellent for saving time editing expense accounts, related vendors, or entire stock lists.

Adding Inventory Products

Now that your inventory tracking is on, it's time to add products for your customers to purchase. Ensure that all parameters are in order before adding stock to your catalog; otherwise, things may become trivial later.

Here are the steps to configure the framework of a product:

1. Click on "Get Paid & Pay"
2. Go to "Products and Services"
3. Add a Name and SKU.
4. Select a Category
5. Choose a Unit (if applicable)

Set up your products correctly, and you'll have less hassle when it comes to tracking sales receipts, invoices, or deposits. Also, you can use **categories** to segment your services or products, making them easier to locate.

Setting Up A Customer Opening Balance

Outstanding supplier and client balances are recorded through this method. If the client had amounts owing after or before the QuickBooks start date, it's a clear sign to set up a customer opening balance.

1. Click 'Customers' after opening "Get Paid & Pay"
2. Pick "New Customer"
3. Enter client credentials
4. Head to the "Payments and Billing" tab, and add the opening balance and the date when the amount is owed.
5. Save the changes

Setting Up A Supplier Opening Balance

Adjust your supplier opening balances in QuickBooks Online with the steps below:

1. Click on 'Expenses'
2. Open 'Suppliers'
3. Choose "New Supplier"
4. Fill in the necessary supplier credentials.
5. Set the **as-of date** and enter the opening balance.
6. Save the New Supplier

Adding A Vendor's Opening Balance

Adding a vendor to your QuickBooks Online account is the same as adding a supplier. Vendors are subcontractors who work for you or people or companies for whom you owe money. Here is how you add a "New Vendor" to your financial roster:

1. Click on "Get Paid & Pay" or 'Expenses'
2. Choose 'Vendors'
3. Navigate to the New Vendor
4. Enter the relevant data on the Vendor information screen.
5. Save your progress

Once the New Vendor is added, you can follow these steps to create an Opening Balance or Unpaid Bill:

1. Select the Vendor you wish to edit

2. Click "New Transaction"

3. Select 'Bill'

4. Compose a new unpaid bill

5. Ensure all the information is correct, including the date and amount owed.

Receiving Payments

There are two ways to record payments within QuickBooks, but ensure you have a clear distinction between them before entering any details.

Invoices

Using an invoice is the correct option if you're selling a service or product and are awaiting future payment. Once the settlement amount is paid (through external means or QuickBooks Payment), you document the transaction in the software.

Sales Receipts

Customers who pay at the time of sale are generally issued sales receipts instead of invoices. You must have already collected payment before sending a new sales receipt to your client. The details are then accounted for in QuickBooks, and the received amount is eliminated.

Undeposited Funds Account

You must process an invoice payment manually after receiving it. First, click '**+New**' and then click "Receive Payment." The money from the paid invoice is then allocated to your Undeposited Funds account.

QuickBooks Online uses this account as a default option that correlates with the Receive Payment feature. The Bank Deposit function allows you to move the payment from the Undeposited Funds account to the correct one.

Sales Tax Specifications

The tax paid may decrease or increase significantly depending on the state where you conduct business. It is the responsibility of all company owners to ensure their enterprise correlates with federal laws.

Updating your sales tax is the first step to collecting the money due for your tax return. Moreover, there are some things you should be aware of before changing your sales tax rate:

- Past transactions are not affected by edits to the tax rate.

- Old invoices remain unchanged unless you edit the individual transaction and adjust the sales tax rate.
- The new rate is implemented if you utilize past data for a new transaction.
- Editing the sales tax rate renders the previous one useless.
- Templates require separate editing if you wish to change or update the sales tax rate.
- Before and after rates are shown if template transactions with both rates are set to a specific time.

Change Your Sales Tax Rate

QuickBooks Online manages the sales tax rates and tax agency information required by the IRS. You can use the software's automated features to your advantage! However, you can still edit this data with the use of custom sales tax rates; here's how:

1. Open 'Taxes.'
2. Click "Sales Tax."
3. Choose "Sales Tax Settings."
4. Edit your amount in the Custom Rate section.
5. Enter the new rate and name.
6. Press 'Continue' and then 'Edit.'

Now that you know how to adjust your sales tax rate accordingly, your business can always stay one step ahead of government institutions.

Additional Customer Contacts

If you have a single client with multiple contact numbers, creating departments within a company or a sub-customer is the solution to this problem. Once you generate a new customer, you'll be able to add sub-customers indefinitely. Here is how to do it:

1. Navigate to the "Customer Center"
2. Choose the name of the Parent Customer
3. Select "Add New Customer"
4. Click "Add Job"
5. Fill in the relevant sub-customers contact details.

6. Press 'Ok'

Now, whenever you are on an invoice, you can select the sub-customer details that fit the data of the current transaction. You'll never have to worry about invoicing a client with more than one telephone number again.

Job Creation In Quickbooks

QuickBooks Online Plus has the Projects feature, which allows you to manage individual jobs with a detailed outline. Once the subscription is updated, you can turn on projects and have total control of them.

1. Locate the New Projects menu on the left of the screen.
2. Click "New Project."
3. Give it a name.
4. Allocate it to a client.
5. Add details or notes.

You can add expenses and income to make it simpler to track the financial analytics of a project. Additional information can be annexed by clicking on the Add to Project button; actions include:

- Invoice
- Receive Payment
- Expense
- Estimate
- Purchase
- Order
- Bill
- Time

With all the tracking data at your fingertips, you'll have a bird's-eye view of your job's inner workings.

Chapter 3:

How to Invoice and Quote

Invoicing Customers

An invoice is a document that provides a detailed description of the products and services you have provided to customers and their respective prices. If the customers do not pay you at the time of the sale, then you need to keep track of what they owe you to ensure that payment is made in the future, so invoices help you manage your account receivable. Invoices are therefore used for sales made on a credit or part payment.

If your business does not use the estimate feature, just start with “create invoices”.

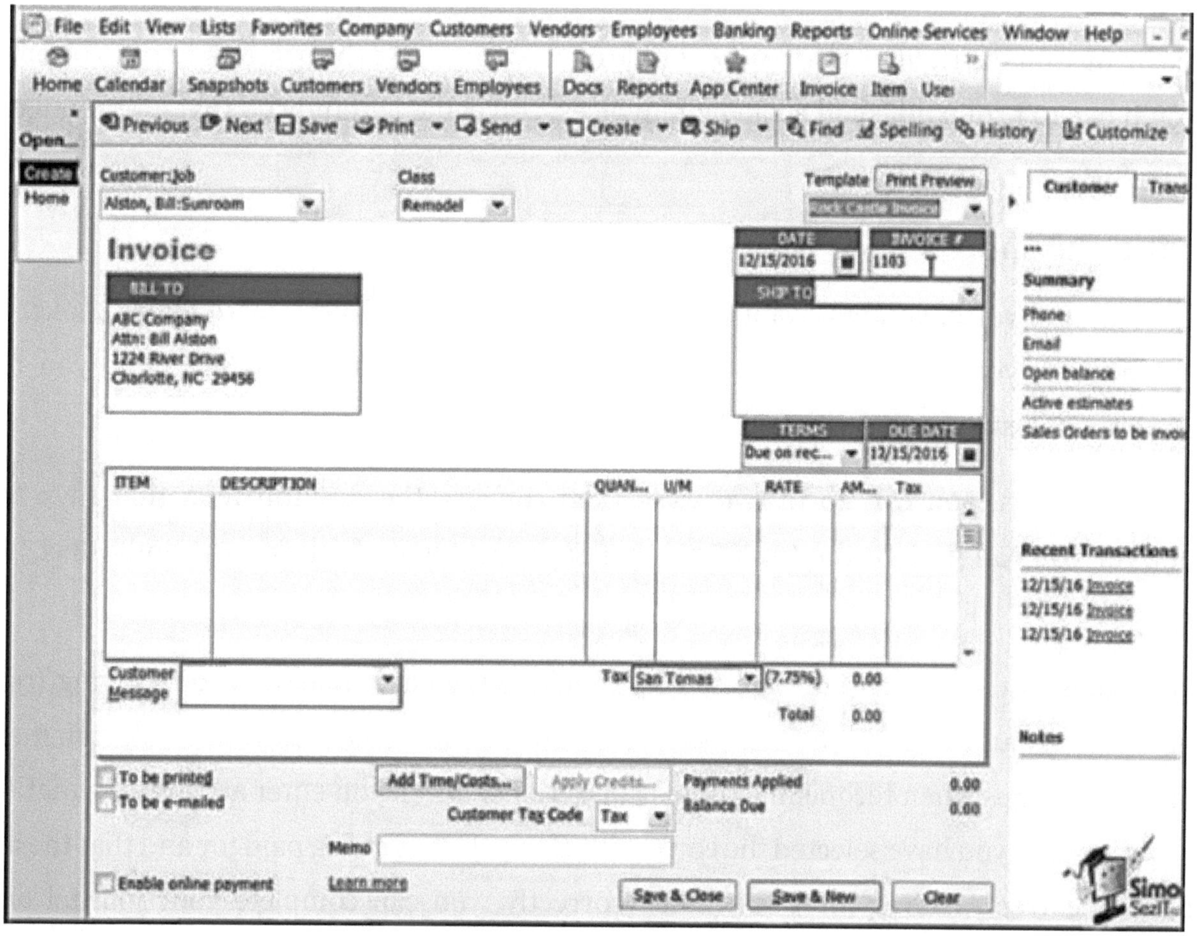

In the invoice window, you will be asked to enter your customer or job, and this information will appear based on how you set up your customer. Next, you will also be required to enter the class you would like to associate this invoice with. After that, you will find the template list. In QuickBooks, you will have several predefined templates for invoices. You do have the ability to customize these or create your own. You will also have to enter the due date for this invoice as other options, such as the invoice date, invoice number, and terms would have already been provided by QuickBooks based on your previous settings.

At the bottom of the invoice, you will be required to enter some details. Under "items", there's a drop-down arrow where you can see the list of available items. Other details to include here are description, quantity, unit of measurement, and tax, and you will also notice that QuickBooks would calculate the quantity times the rate to give you the amount.

Below your items, you will see your Customer message window. Here, you can include an appreciation note to your customers. To the right, you will see the sales tax rate that this particular customer is charged. So you will notice it tells you the actual rate and the amount of sales tax charged on the total invoice. Below this, you will see the total amount of the invoice itself.

Below the invoice on the right, you will see a couple of checkboxes, "to be printed" and "to be emailed". If you would like to print and email a batch of invoices, you could certainly do that and email or print them all at once.

Receiving Payments

After creating an invoice, you will want to get paid, and you can do this with QuickBooks. This is important because you need to ensure you are not working for free, and secondly, you need to reconcile your bank statements with QuickBooks.

To receive payments, you can go in two ways. You can use the desktop Icon that says "receive Payments," or you can go into the top menu that says "customers", click on it and select "receive payments".

Enter the details in the appropriate boxes. These include the customer you are receiving from, the payment amount, and the payment method. Make sure the date matches your bank statements, so you do not have issues when reconciling these transactions. When you enter all this information, you need to confirm that you have selected the correct invoice you are getting paid for and that the amount you receive is correct. If everything is entered correctly, you can complete your journal entry by clicking "save and close or save and new".

I suggest you check your accounts receivable reports weekly to keep track.

Paying Vendors

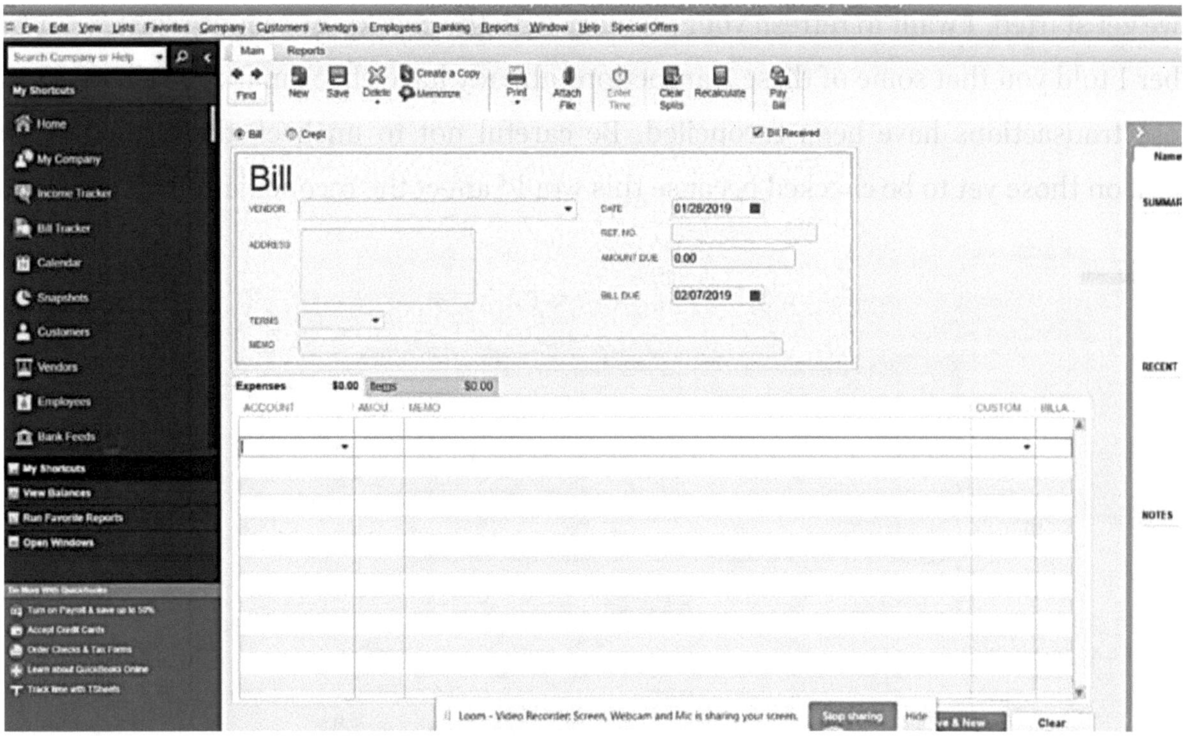

There are two options you can use to pay bills. On the home screen of the QuickBooks desktop, you can simply click the “pay bills” button or click the vendor drop-down menu at the top of the screen and pay bills. Either way, it will take you to the same place.

When you proceed to pay bills, it brings up the screen with all the bills entered into the company file. You can do certain things on this screen.

At the top of the screen, you have the option to show all bills or shows bills due on or before a certain date. You can choose to pay all bills or pay some selected bills. Also, if you want to make a partial payment, you simply highlight and enter the amount you are ready to pay, and below it, QuickBook will indicate that you still have an amount due to this company.

Below the bills tab, you will see a couple of other things. It’s going to show if you have discounts that can be used. If you have credits with this vendor, you can set the credits against the bills you are paying. The payment method is very important, so you need to set up your payments. You need to make sure your payment comes from the right account. If you are paying by cheque, make sure it is coming from your cheque account. So whether you pay through cheque, credit cards, or online payment, after picking the payment method, click “pay selected bills”, and a screen will pop up for more details, after which you are done.

Reconciling Your Accounts

Before we get started, I want to refresh your memory with the checking account register, and you will remember I told you that some of these transactions already have check marks on them. This means that those transactions have been reconciled. Be careful not to uncheck these and not to put a checkmark on those yet to be checked because this would affect the reconciliation.

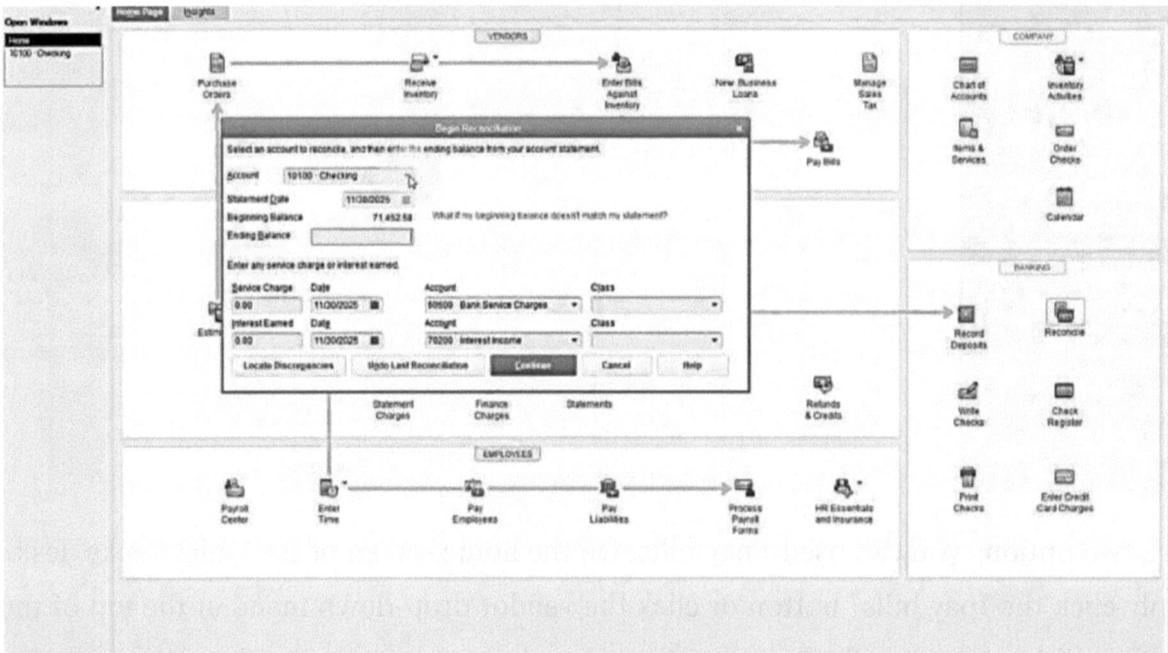

On the home screen of your Desktop, click on "reconcile". You will first tell QuickBooks which account you are trying to reconcile and then make sure your statement date matches the date on your bank statement. You will also notice that you cannot change the number in the beginning balance box. If you reconciled last month, then last month's ending number is this month's beginning number. If you know you reconciled last month, and this is different when you come in to do this month, then you should locate your discrepancies below. This runs and reports and shows you anything you changed since you last reconciled. What may have happened is that you've unchecked something in the register or deleted a transaction you already reconciled.

If you have a service charge, make sure to plug that in and choose the correct account in the account section. If you have any earned interest, create an account called interest income. If you use the class feature, choose the right class.

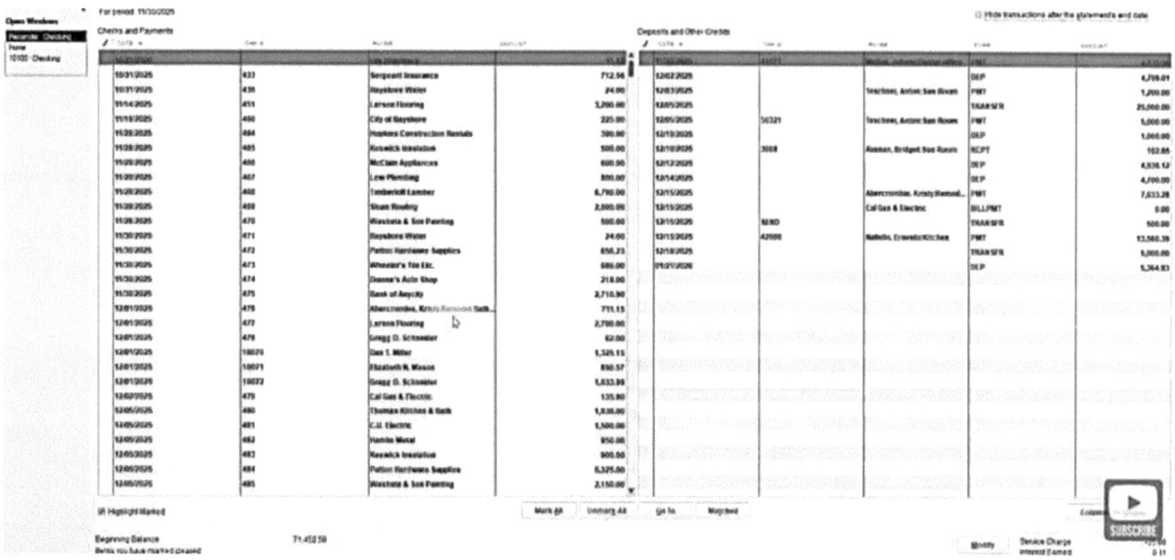

When you hit continue, it will open up another window. The way this window is laid out, you will notice on the left is anything that came out of the bank account, and on the right is anything that went into the bank account. Your job is to look at the bank statement. If it is on the statement, check it off; if not, do not check it off. This is a great way to see if you missed entering something, entered something twice, or even put in the wrong amount. To make any changes, double-click the transaction, after which you save it.

When you look down at the bottom, it will tell you the total of your check, and you should ensure that it is the same number on your bank statement. If these two numbers match your bank statement, it is balanced. If you see the zero difference, that's what you want. If it is anything other than zero, you are not balanced.

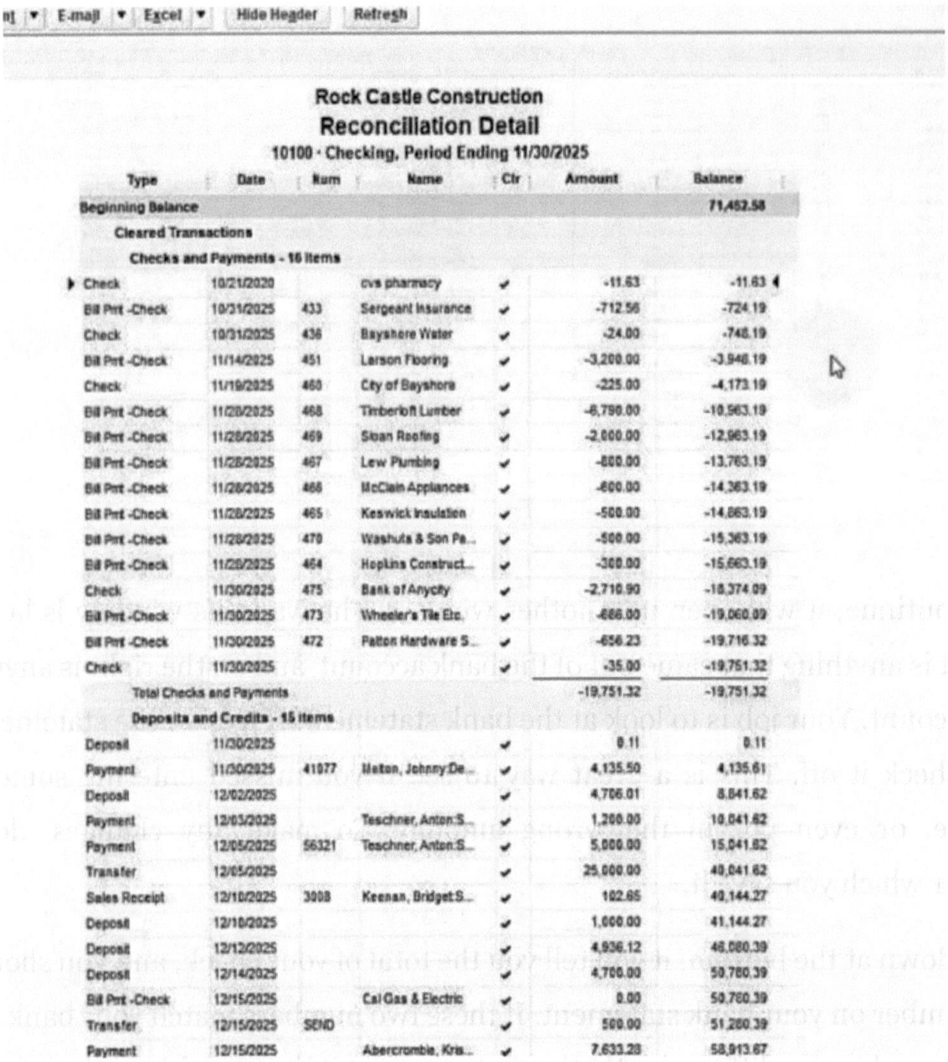

Rock Castle Construction

Reconciliation Detail

10100 · Checking, Period Ending 11/30/2025

Type	Date	Num	Name	Clr	Amount	Balance
Beginning Balance						71,452.58
Cleared Transactions						
Checks and Payments - 16 items						
Check	10/21/2020		cvs pharmacy	✔	-11.63	-11.63
Bill Pmt -Check	10/31/2025	433	Sergeant Insurance	✔	-712.56	-724.19
Check	10/31/2025	436	Bayshore Water	✔	-24.00	-748.19
Bill Pmt -Check	11/14/2025	451	Larson Flooring	✔	-3,200.00	-3,948.19
Check	11/19/2025	460	City of Bayshore	✔	-225.00	-4,173.19
Bill Pmt -Check	11/20/2025	468	Timberloft Lumber	✔	-6,790.00	-10,963.19
Bill Pmt -Check	11/28/2025	469	Sloan Roofing	✔	-2,000.00	-12,963.19
Bill Pmt -Check	11/28/2025	467	Lew Plumbing	✔	-800.00	-13,763.19
Bill Pmt -Check	11/28/2025	466	McClain Appliances	✔	-600.00	-14,363.19
Bill Pmt -Check	11/28/2025	465	Keswick Insulation	✔	-500.00	-14,863.19
Bill Pmt -Check	11/28/2025	470	Washuta & Son Pa...	✔	-500.00	-15,363.19
Bill Pmt -Check	11/28/2025	464	Hopkins Construct...	✔	-300.00	-15,663.19
Check	11/30/2025	475	Bank of Anycity	✔	-2,710.90	-18,374.09
Bill Pmt -Check	11/30/2025	473	Wheeler's Tile Etc.	✔	-686.00	-19,060.09
Bill Pmt -Check	11/30/2025	472	Patton Hardware S...	✔	-656.23	-19,716.32
Check	11/30/2025			✔	-35.00	-19,751.32
Total Checks and Payments					-19,751.32	-19,751.32
Deposits and Credits - 15 items						
Deposit	11/30/2025			✔	0.11	0.11
Payment	11/30/2025	41977	Melton, Johnny:De...	✔	4,135.50	4,135.61
Deposit	12/02/2025			✔	4,706.01	8,841.62
Payment	12/03/2025		Teschner, Anton:S...	✔	1,200.00	10,041.62
Payment	12/05/2025	56321	Teschner, Anton:S...	✔	5,000.00	15,041.62
Transfer	12/05/2025			✔	25,000.00	40,041.62
Sales Receipt	12/10/2025	3008	Keenan, Bridget:S...	✔	102.65	40,144.27
Deposit	12/10/2025			✔	1,000.00	41,144.27
Deposit	12/12/2025			✔	4,936.12	46,080.39
Deposit	12/14/2025			✔	4,700.00	50,780.39
Bill Pmt -Check	12/15/2025		Cal Gas & Electric	✔	0.00	50,780.39
Transfer	12/15/2025	SEND		✔	500.00	51,280.39
Payment	12/15/2025		Abercrombie, Kris...	✔	7,633.28	58,913.67

When done, you may be prompted to run reconciliation reports, and you can decide whether to print them or not.

Make sure to reconcile all your bank accounts, credit cards, and other accounts to ensure you are in balance.

Chapter 4:

Sales and Receipts

How To Record A Full Payment

There are numerous ways to reach the screen for recording payments. The New button in the left-hand Navigation Pane is one option. Under Customers, click the Receive Payment link.

This time, we'll try a different method, which involves navigating to Sales in the Navigation Pane and clicking on Customers. Here you may see that our customer has an outstanding balance and a link to receive payment.

When we click to receive payment, the Receive Payment form is automatically populated with our customer's information.

We can locate the relevant invoice via invoice number. However, this customer's invoices are already included in the Outstanding Transactions list at the bottom of the page.

Choose the date when the consumer sent money for the Payment Date field.

Next, we must choose a Payment Method. Numerous payment options are available, including credit card, cash, cheque, and PayPal.

Simply select the Add New link in the drop-down menu to add more payment methods. For instance, you can enter Bitcoin, which will immediately display as an option.

You may include a payment reference number.

Select Undeposited Funds for the Deposit to account option. You may deposit funds into another account, such as a checking or savings account. If you anticipate additional deposits, keeping the contribution in Undeposited Funds may be preferable.

Then, input the customer's payment amount. QuickBooks Online will enter the whole amount by default. However, a consumer may not have submitted all of that information.

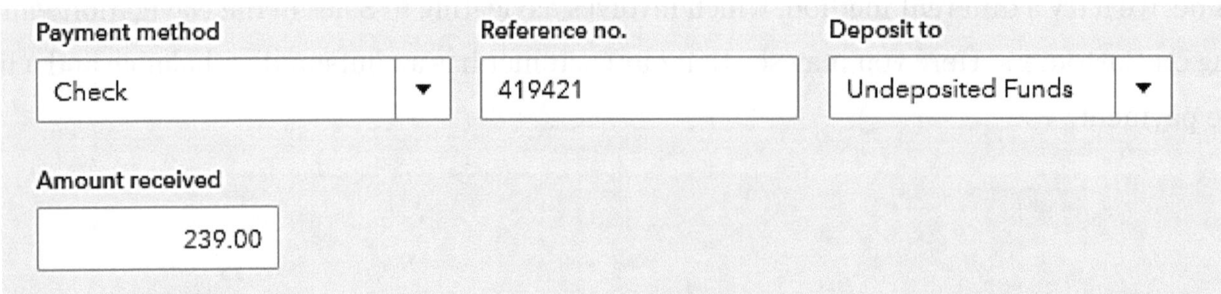

Now we must review the client bills in the list of Outstanding Transactions. This table has five columns: Description, Due Date, Original Amount, Open Balance, and Payment.

If the customer has only one outstanding invoice and sends the payment amount, it is straightforward to apply the money to that invoice.

Occasionally, a customer will have multiple open invoices and send insufficient funds to cover them. QuickBooks applies the payment to the oldest invoice first by default.

Specify the particular amounts in the Payment column if you need to pay the invoices in a different sequence.

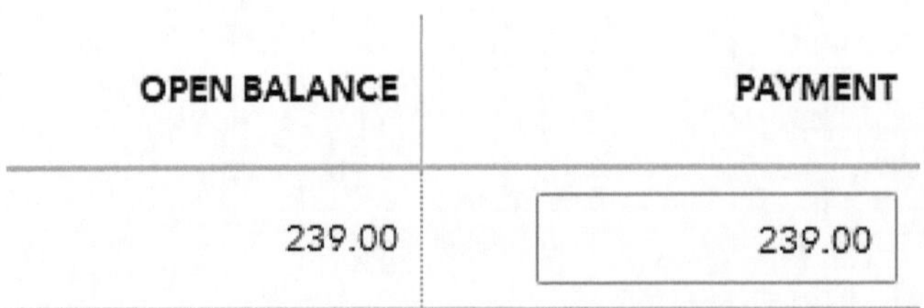

You can see the entire amount that will be applied beneath the table. If credit memos are available, they could be applied here as well.

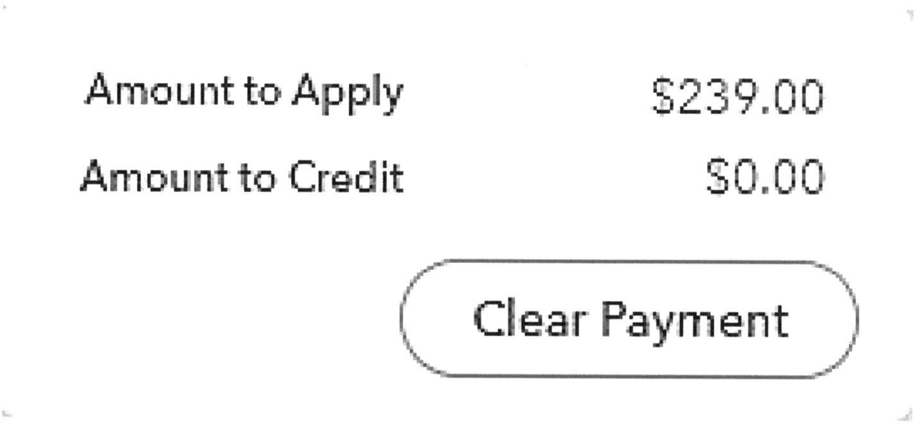

A memo and attachment can also be included in the Receive Payment form.

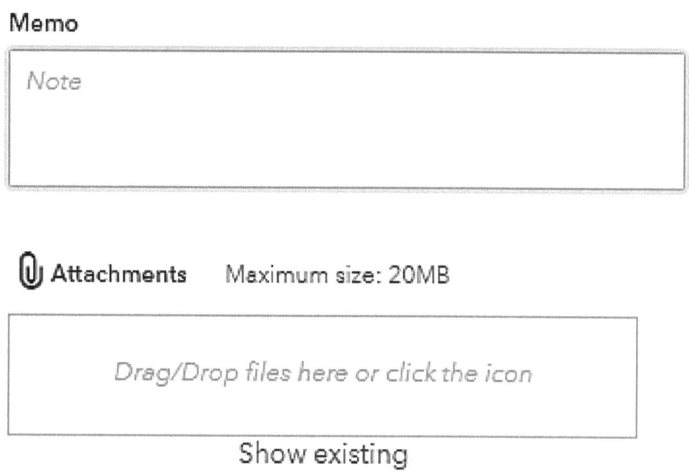

After completing the form, you can save it and proceed. You have the options Save and New, Save and Close, and Save and Send at the bottom of the page.

Save, and New will save the payment and launch a brand-new, blank Receive Payment form. This will save the payment and return you to the previous screen. Store and save the payment and provide the option to send it as a PDF file. After saving the file, the payment will be processed, which you can confirm.

How To Enter A Partial Payment

- Select **add transaction** after navigating to transactions.
- Input the date of the partial payment and indicate that it is a partial payment in the notes or description section.
- Enter the amount and then click on a category to pick it.
- Click on **income**, then click **Save.**

- After completing QuickBooks accept payment for an invoice, repeat the preceding steps and mention the purpose of the payment under the description or notes. You may alternatively wait until you get the whole money before marking the transaction as paid.

Apply One Payment To Multiple Invoices

- To apply a single payment to numerous QuickBooks invoices, choose "**Customers> Receive Payments**" from the menu.
- Then, choose the recipient from the **"Received From" drop-down menu.**
- Choose the payment date from the "Date" calendar picker.
- Enter the single payment amount into the "Amount" column.
- Then, click the button corresponding to the mode of payment received.
- If necessary, click the drop-down menu on the lower-right side of this button group to view more payment methods. Choose a payment option from the drop-down menu.
- Choose a credit card type from the "Payment" drop-down menu to enter "Credit/Debit" payments.
- Afterwards, input the expiration date and credit card number in the "Card Number" and "Expiration Date" fields of the resulting drop-down menu.
- To save the credit card, click the "Done" button in the drop-down menu.
- Insert the check number into the "Check No." section when recording a check. QuickBooks applies the single payment to the outstanding invoices in reverse chronological order.
- Click the "Un-Apply Payment" button on the "Main" tab of the Ribbon to remove the checkmarks from the invoices (s).
- Also, check and uncheck the invoices by clicking in the column with the leftmost checkmark to apply and remove payment amounts, as necessary.
- Repeat step 13 until the total amount is assigned to the appropriate invoices in the correct quantities.
- Change the amounts in the "Payment" column to the right of the invoices to adjust the amounts applied to each invoice.
- To save your changes and close the "Receive Payments" window, click "Save & Close."
- Click "Save & New" instead to save the transaction while leaving the "Receive Payments" window open.

How To Make Deposits

Once you're eager to deposit at the bank, either in person or via your mobile device, you must also make a similar transaction in QuickBooks. So that you can match downloaded transactions and reconcile your account at the end of the month, the deposited amount in QuickBooks must correspond to what was deposited in the bank.

To create a Deposit, simply;

- Select the Create button (+) before choosing Bank Deposit.
- At the upper part of the Deposit screen, be careful to pick the right bank account you are depositing.
- Enter the Date when the deposit was made or will be made.
- Choose the Payments to include in the deposit from the received payments list.
- Add any additional deposits to the Add New Deposits lines located beneath the list of payments.
- Ensure that the deposit amount matches the amount you brought to the bank or will bring.
- Click Save and Close or Save and New.

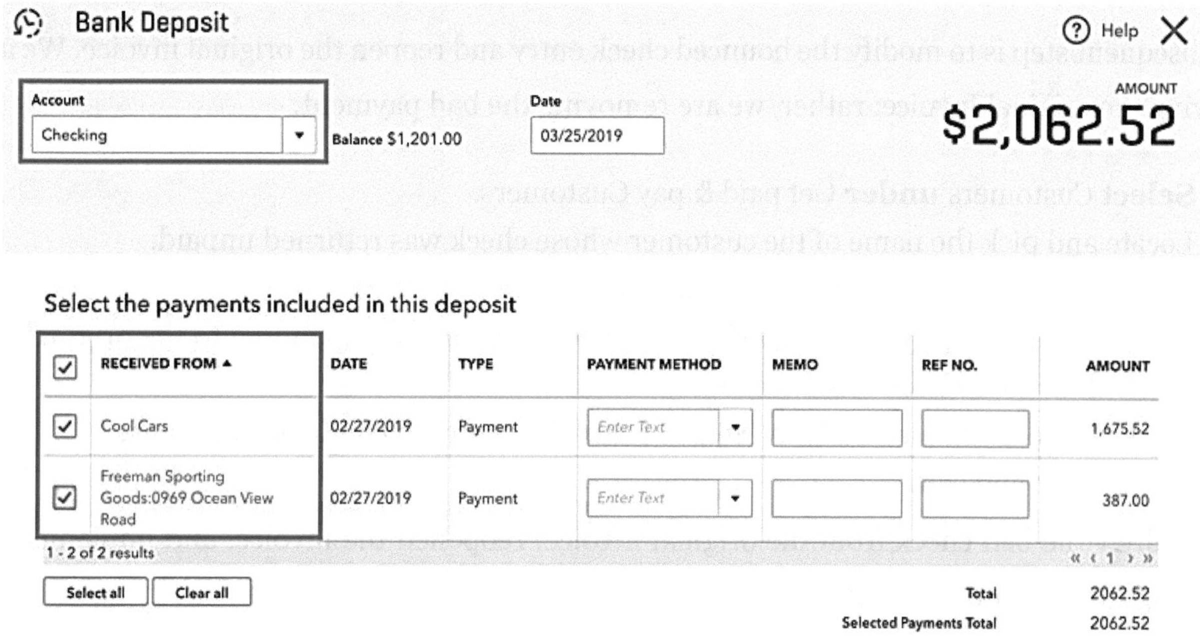

Congratulations! You now understand how to record deposits correctly in QuickBooks Online.

Handling Bounced Checks

Let us assume a customer's check bounces, and the accounting can be handled in several ways.

These procedures are difficult. If you are uncertain, contact your accountant. This can become complicated, but they understand how to handle the following steps.

Step 1: Insert the amount of the returned check as a cost

First, the bounced check must be recorded as an expense:

- Choose + **New.**
- Select **Expense.**
- Click on the name of the customer whose check bounced in the Payee section.

- In the Payment Account drop-down menu, select the account where the funds should have been deposited.
- In the Payment date field, put the date you discovered the cheque to have insufficient funds.
- Choose and expand the Category details drop-down menu.
- Select **Accounts Receivable** from the Category field.
- Indicate the amount of the returned check in the Amount column.
- Enter a comment in the Description section, such as "bouncing check" or "NSF check."
- When finished, select **Save** and Exit.

This expense offsets the invoice that remains unpaid.

Step 2: Remove the returned check from the original invoice.

The subsequent step is to modify the bounced check entry and reopen the original invoice. We are not modifying the original invoice; rather, we are removing the bad payment:

- **Select** Customers **under** Get paid & pay Customers.
- Locate and pick the name of the customer whose check was returned unpaid.
- Locate and pick the record for the check that bounced.
- In the **Received payment window**, uncheck the box corresponding to the original invoice to which the bad check was attached.
- Mark the item you just made in "Step 1: Enter the returned check as an expense."
- Select **Save** and exit.

You withdrew the bad check from the original invoice, reopened the invoice, and implemented the accounting from Step 1. To double-check:

- Select Customers under **Get paid & pay Customers**.
- Locate and pick the name of the customer whose check was returned unpaid.
- Check the Status column next to the original invoice. Now it should read "Open."

Step 3: Create an item for bounced check fees charged by your bank

Hint: You only need to configure the item once. If you've done this before, proceed directly to Step 4.

Create a service item for returned checks and associated fees. This enables you to include them in invoices you can send to your customers.

Create two items, one for the bank's fee and the other for the amount you wish to charge the customer for returned check costs.

- Navigate to Settings.

- Select **Products and services** under Lists.
- Choose **New.**
- Select **Service** in the Product/Service information panel.
- In the Name field, Insufficient type Funds.
- Select the bank account the returned check was made on from the list of Income accounts.
- To create a new item, select **Save and new.**
- Identify the second item with the **bounced checks fee**
- Select or add a Bounced Check Fees income account from the drop-down list of Income accounts.
- Alternatively, you can select a separate spending account to track your bank fees.
- Select **Save** and exit.

Step 4: Enter the service fee charged by your bank.

Since the bank charged you, you must still record this spending in your financial records:

- Choose + **New.**
- Under **Vendors**, select **Expense.**
- Select your bank from the Payment account dropdown list.
- In the Payment date field, put the date the cheque was returned for insufficient funds.
- Enter the NSF charge in Ref no.
- Select the Bank Charges expenditure account from the drop-down menu under **Category** Details.
- In the Amount column, enter the amount your bank charged you for the returned check.
- Select **Save** and exit.

This logs the bank service fee so that you have a record of who paid for what.

Step 5: Create an invoice for the returned check fees and mail it to the customer.

You now have a record of not getting the funds, the fees the bank charged you, and an "open" and unpaid invoice for the original customer.

Now you can resend the original invoice to the client, as it remains unpaid.

Create a new invoice if you wish to charge the customer for the bounced check fees as well. It is vital that the original invoice not be altered.

- Choose + **New.**
- In the Customers section, select **Invoice.**
- In the **Invoice date column,** select the Customer's name and enter the date the check bounced.

- In the **Product/Service column,** select the item you created for Bounced check fees from the drop-down menu.
- Enter the amount charged to the client for the returned check. Enter a note in the Message on the statement field. Explain to the customer the nature & purpose of this charge.
- Select **Save** and exit.

Step 6: Send your customer a statement

Lastly, send your customer a statement. This summarises what they owe you and why they owe you.

- Customers can be accessed by going to **Get paid & pay or Sales**, then selecting **Customers**.
- Choose the name of the customer who issued the bounced check on the Customers page to see the Transaction List.
- Choose **Statement** from the drop-down menu labeled **New transaction.**
- Select the **desired Statement Type** from the drop-down menu.
- Set the Date of the Statement, the Start Date, and the End Date.
- Investigate the **Description column**. You will notice your explanation of why you are sending them the second invoice.
- Choose **Print** to create a copy of the invoice, or select **Save and send** to attach the invoice to an email, then send it to the customer.

After you send the invoice or statement to the consumer, they understand what they owe and why. The statement informs the customer that there is still an open invoice and a second invoice to cover the bank fees & any fees you are charging for the bounced check.

Chapter 5:

Bank Accounts

One of the most convenient features of QuickBooks Online is connecting your bank accounts (also called Bank Feeds) and credit cards to automatically pull data from your bank and credit card company. The power to connect your accounts will eliminate stacks of data entry, saving you a lot of time and frustration. If done correctly, your books will be kept up to date, allowing you to make quicker business decisions with real-time figures.

Setting Up Bank Accounts

There are two ways to connect your bank accounts to QuickBooks Online. The first way is to automatically link your bank accounts to pull your data into QuickBooks Online. This is the most convenient and constant way to sync your data. Unfortunately, not all banks are set up to be connected to QuickBooks Online, so this feature may not be an option depending on your bank.

The second way to pull your bank data is to import your transactions via downloading a .csv file from your bank and importing the transactions to QuickBooks Online. This is not the recommended approach, but depending on your bank, it may be the only option. It's just going to take a couple more steps.

Let's start with how to automatically connect your account and import transactions manually.

Automatically Connect Bank Account To Quickbooks Online

Connecting your bank accounts is a simple and convenient way to keep your books updated. QuickBooks Online does all the heavy lifting and will memorize transactions as you work in the books. This saves you a ton of time and then creates more accurate and reliable financials. For example, if you code a Starbucks expense to Meals & Entertainment, the next time you visit Starbucks, QuickBooks Online will automatically code that expense to Meals & Entertainment, giving you more time to enjoy your vanilla latte.

Here are the steps to connect your bank to import your transactions automictically:

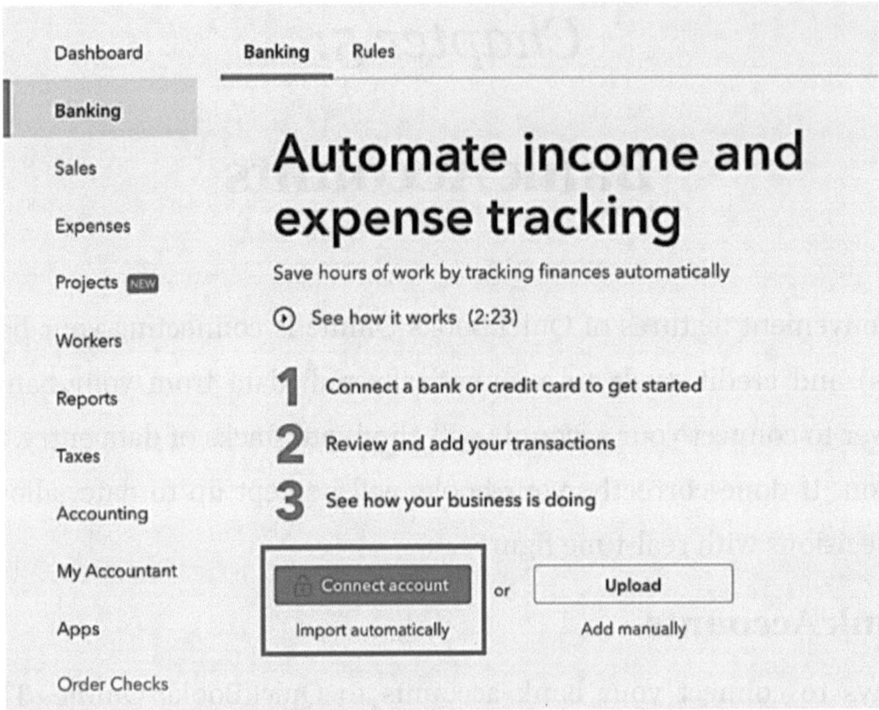

QuickBooks Online allows users to automatically connect bank and credit card accounts to pull account info.

1. Under the "Bank Accounts" section on your **Dashboard**, select *Connect Account.*
2. Enter your bank name or select your bank from the images on the screen.

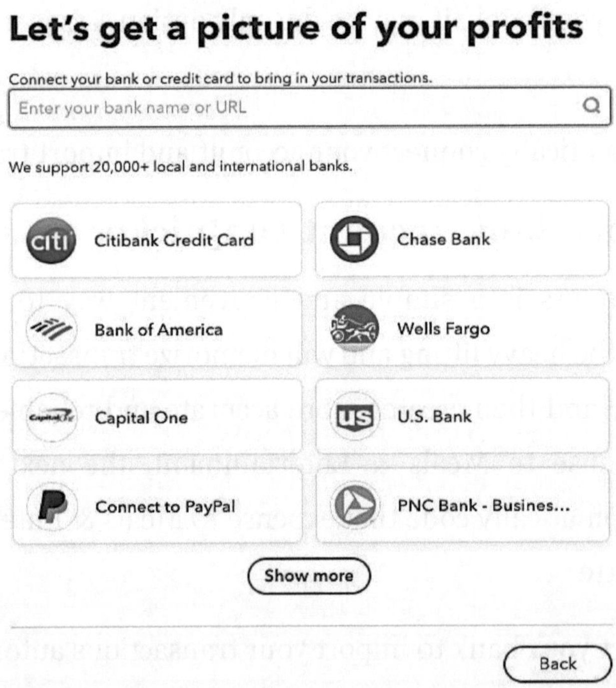

QuickBooks Online links with most major banks and credit card companies. Use the search bar to find your bank if it's not included in the icon listing.

3. Enter your bank username and password on your bank's home screen.
4. Select the account you wish to connect to QuickBooks Online and select Connect.
5. QuickBooks Online will automatically connect to your bank account and transfer the prior three months (or 90 days) of activity.

Note that if you have multiple accounts with the bank, you can select the accounts you wish to link or connect all the accounts.

Manually Importing Bank Activity Into Quickbooks Online

If your bank does not allow linking your bank accounts, you need to download your bank activity from your bank's website manually. Let's discuss how to plan and execute a successful import of your bank activity.

Before you head over to your bank's website to find your data, it's important that you review the dates for which your data is already updated through. You will want to return to a reasonable starting point if you have never input information from your bank account in QuickBooks Online. This could be the inception of the business if you just started or the beginning of the year if you have been in business but are new to QuickBooks Online. Here is how to view your account register and find the latest transactions:

1. Start by going to the chart of accounts by selecting the *Settings* icon (⚙), then *Chart of Accounts*.
2. Find the bank account that you want to add additional activity to. If this is a new bank account, add the account to your Chart of Accounts.
3. Under the "Action" column, select *View register*.
4. The first transaction will typically be the latest and your starting point when downloading activity from your bank.

It's recommended that you write down the date range that you wish to download and import while you are still in your books and can review your transaction history quickly.

Now let's head over to your bank's website and follow these simple steps:

5. Log into your bank's website.

6. Find where to download transactions. This is often found in the account activity detail section of the bank's website, but this depends on the bank.
7. Select to download the QuickBooks Online file. Some banks may also offer a .csv file which will work as well.
8. Select the correct date range based on the last transaction you recorded in the prior section. Most banks will allow you to customize the date range and specify the transactions you want to download.
9. Download and save your QuickBooks Online transaction file somewhere safe, like your computer's desktop.

Now that you have the file downloaded from your bank, you are ready to upload the transactions into your QuickBooks Online account. Follow these steps to upload your transactions:

1. Start by selecting the *Settings* icon (⚙), then *Import data* under the "Tools" column.
2. Select *Bank Data* from the import data options.

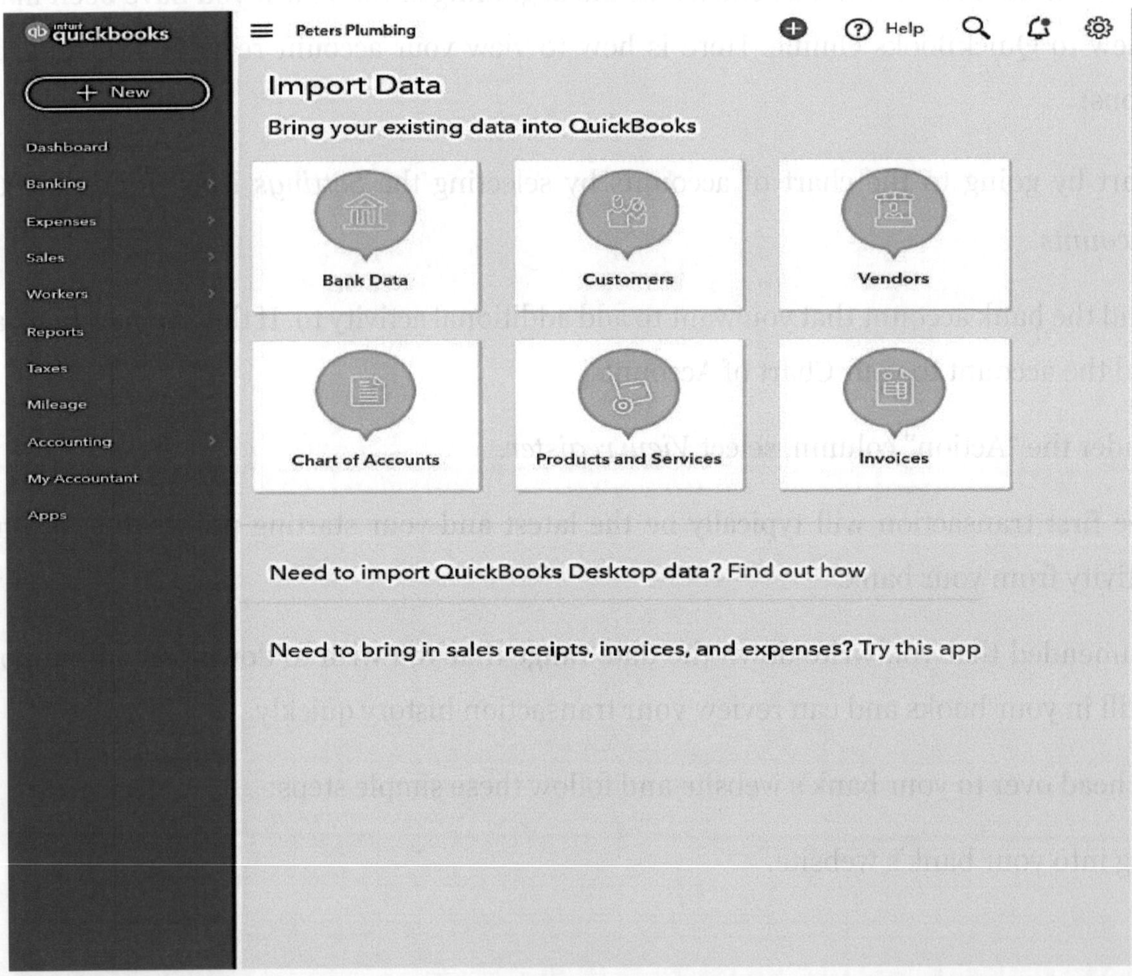

Importing data lets you quickly load large files, avoiding time-consuming data entry.

3. Under the "Get your info from your bank" option, use the *Browse* button to find your QuickBooks Online or .csv file on your computer.

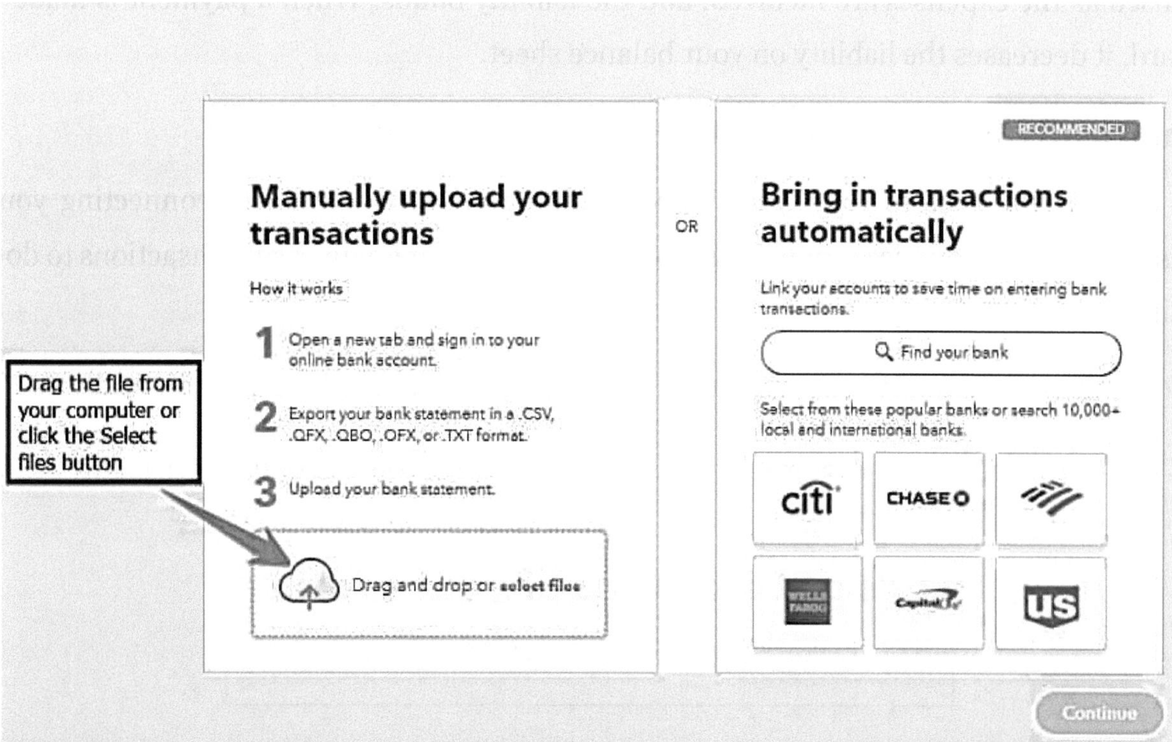

Manually uploading transactions can be time-consuming, as you must download the transactions from your bank and upload them. The preferred method is to link your accounts and automatically pull in transactions.

4. Next, select the account you wish to import your data into in the Account drop-down. (This should be the QuickBooks Online account related to this bank account.)

5. Finally, select *Let's Go*, and the import will begin.

Once your transactions have been imported into QuickBooks Online, it's time to categorize your expenses into the correct accounts from your chart of accounts. In the next section, we will go over how to connect your credit cards; then, we will dive into categorizing your transactions.

Credit Card Setup

Setting up your credit cards is very similar to your bank accounts. Like your bank accounts, there are two ways to connect your credit cards, automatically and manually. Credit cards can be a bit trickier if there is more than one card on the account, and often the dates on credit cards do not follow a traditional month. Credit cards' monthly close date is often in the middle of the month, so it's important to double-check the dates before importing data into your books to avoid duplicating activity.

The credit card activity will appear as a liability on your balance sheet. Your credit card activity will be expensed as the expenses are incurred, and the liability builds. When a payment is made to your credit card, it decreases the liability on your balance sheet.

Automatically Connect Credit Card To Quickbooks Online

Adding your credit cards to your QuickBooks Online account is similar to connecting your bank accounts. Connecting your account will automatically allow your credit card transactions to download in real time.

Here are the steps to connect your credit card to import your transactions automictically:

1. Under the "Bank Accounts" section on your **Dashboard**, select *Connect Accounts*.

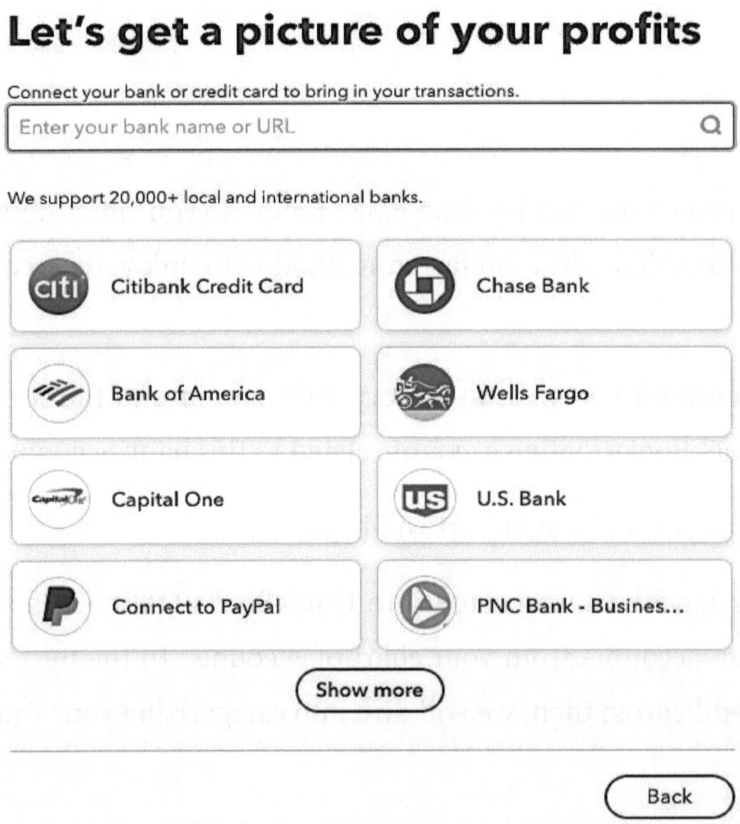

QuickBooks Online will allow for automatic connectivity from most major banks.

2. Enter your financial institution or select your bank from the images on the screen.

3. Enter your credit card login information (username and password) on your creditor's home screen.

4. Select the account you wish to connect to QuickBooks Online and select Connect.
5. QuickBooks Online will automatically connect to your bank account and transfer the prior three months (or 90 days) of activity.

Note that if you have multiple credit card accounts with a company, you can select the accounts you wish to link or choose to link all the accounts. Make sure not to link your accounts, as you don't want to co-mingle your business and personal credit card activity.

Manually Import Credit Card Activity To Quickbooks Online

If your credit card company does allow for the linking of your accounts, then you will need to manually download your activity from your credit card company's website.

Credit cards often have statement dates that do not align with a typical calendar month. This makes double-checking the dates before downloading even more important. Here is how to view your account register and find the latest transactions:

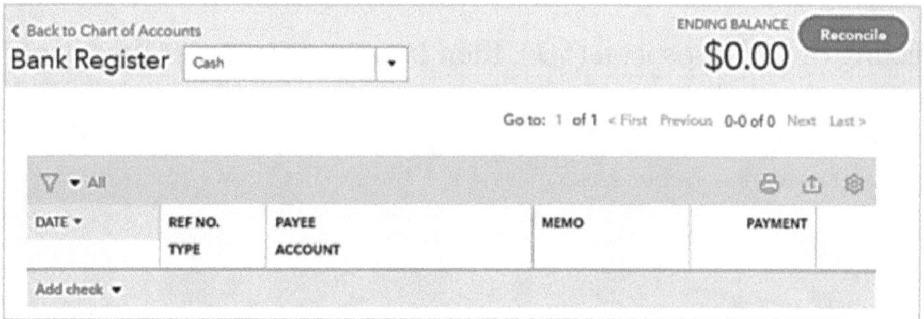

Finding the starting point for downloading transactions is key to avoiding duplication of activity.

1. Start by going to the chart of accounts by selecting the *Settings* icon (⚙), then *Chart of Accounts*.
2. Find the credit card account that you want to add additional activity to. If this is a new credit card account, add the account to your Chart of Accounts.
3. Under the "Action" column, select *View register*.
4. The first transaction will typically be the latest and your starting point when downloading activity from your credit card.
5. Make sure to write down the date range you wish to download and import while you are still in your books and can review the transaction history.

It's now time to head over to your credit card company's website and follow these simple steps:

1. Log into your credit card website.
2. Find where to download transactions on your credit card website.
3. Select to download the QuickBooks Online file. Some banks may also offer a CVS file which will work as well.
4. Select the correct date range based on the last transaction in the prior section. Most credit card companies will allow you to customize the date range and specify the transaction rate you want to download.
5. Download and save your QuickBooks Online transaction file somewhere safe, like your computer's desktop.

It's now time to upload the transactions into your QuickBooks Online account. Open your QuickBooks Online account and follow these steps to upload your transactions:

1. Start by selecting the *Settings* icon (⚙), then *Import data* under the "Tools" column.

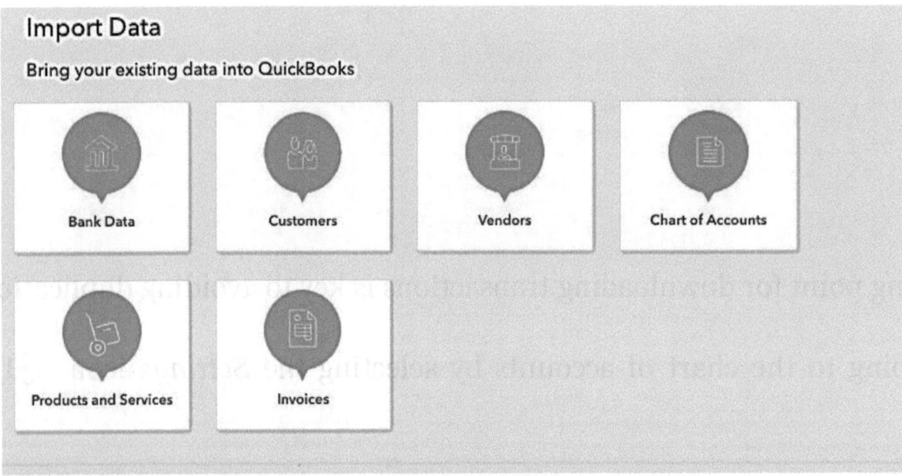

Linking accounts will avoid the duplication of activity in your accounts.

2. Select Bank Data from the import data options.
3. Under the "Get your info from your Bank" option, use the *Browse* button to find your QuickBooks Online or CSV file on your computer.
4. Next, select the account where you wish to import your data in the Account drop-down. (This should be the QuickBooks Online account related to this credit card account.)
5. Finally, select *Let's Go*, and the import will begin.

Now that your credit card transactions have been imported into QuickBooks Online, it's time to categorize your income and expenses into the correct accounts from your chart of accounts. In the next section, we will review how to categorize your income and expenses and set up rules so QuickBooks Online will automatically recognize and categorize transactions.

Categorizing Bank Activity

Now that you have all your bank and credit card activity imported to QuickBooks Online, we need to ensure it ends up in the right location. Properly categorizing your data will ensure accurate and reliable financials. Matching transactions can take some time, but it's important to put the time up-front to ensure your books are accurate for years to come. The more time spent confirming that your data is correct, the more time and frustration you will save yourself down the road.

The process of matching and categorizing your data starts by reviewing the imported data and then matching each item to an account. For example, if you purchased some paper and supplies from Staples, you would use the drop-down menu to select the "Office Supplies" account. This can be done manually, and QuickBooks Online will automatically match your data as you work through the software.

The first step is reviewing the data you just imported into QuickBooks Online. In the "Banking" section, you will see your bank account activity and credit card activity that has been imported.

Follow these steps to review your imported bank/credit card activity:

1. From the home screen, use the left-hand menu to select *Banking*.
2. Select the account for which you want to categorize activity. You can also switch accounts by using the drop-down option.
3. Select the For Review tab.

Once transactions are categorized, they will be moved to the Categorized tab, where they can still be adjusted before being finalized.

Once you reach the Review tab, you will see several columns with transaction details, including Date, Description, Payee, Category or Match, Spent, Received, and Action. You will want to review each transaction individually to ensure it has the correct Payee and is in the correct category. QuickBooks Online will try to automatically match your transactions to categories based on your historical entries. QuickBooks Online calls this "Matching." Remember that it's still important to review each transaction to confirm it's been properly sorted. The more you categorize your data, the less work you will be required to do, as QuickBooks Online learns your income and expense sources and where they should be categorized.

Adding New Transactions

To add new transactions, you'll first want to review and edit the *Payee* and *Category* before adding each transaction to your books. Each transaction's date, description, and the amount should pull in automatically from your import. You must add the Payee and select the "Category" for each transaction. Here are the steps to review each transaction:

1. Select the transaction you wish to edit and approve.

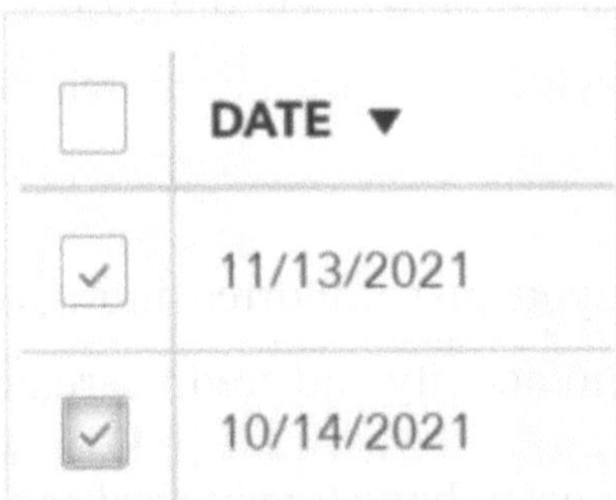

Select the transaction you wish to include in the approval.

2. Select the vendor or customer from the Vendor/Customer listing. If your vendor or customer is not already in QuickBooks Online, you need to manually set them up by selecting *Add new* at the top of the drop-down menu.

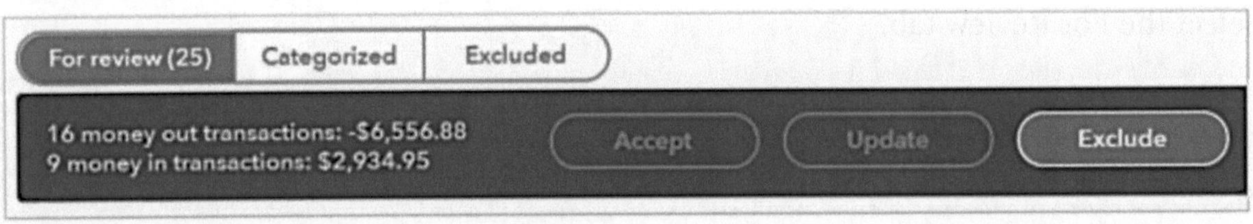

Accept, update, or exclude the transactions from your listing.

3. Select the "Category" from the drop-down menu. The categories are your accounts from your chart of accounts. To add a new account, scroll to the top of the drop-down menu and select *Add new*.

4. Once finished, select *Add*.

Once you have reviewed and added a transaction, you can still edit or undo your activity by selecting the Categorized tab above the transaction details. You can undo a transaction by selecting *Undo* in the "Action" column, and the transaction will be moved back to the For Review tab.

Matching Transactions

One of the best timesaving features of QuickBooks Online is the matching feature. QuickBooks Online will match deposits, checks, vendors, and account classifications. QuickBooks Online will automatically remember your coding selections for certain transactions and auto-populate the account information for your review. You will still need to review the populated data and either approve the match or edit it before approval.

Follow these steps to match transactions:

1. Select *Banking* from the left-hand menu.
2. Select the For Review tab under the account you are categorizing activity in.
3. Under the "Action" column, look for the word "Match".
4. Review and confirm the matched data for accuracy. If the data is correct, select *Match* under the "Action" column. If the data is incorrect, select the account and edit the category.

Once you have reviewed and matched the transactions, the data will be active in QuickBooks Online. While accepting data and making edits to the classifications, you can always review transactions that have been accepted or matched by going to the Categorized tab. Additionally, you can approve multiple transactions at once by selecting the box next to each transaction you wish to approve and selecting *Accept* from the menu above the data.

Working With Registers

Registers are similar to a checkbook register you may use to track your bank account activity. QuickBooks Online can view all the activity in a particular balance sheet account. You can view the details of an account and edit individual transactions.

Follow these steps to view the register:

1. Start by selecting the *Settings* icon (⚙).
2. Under the "Your Company" column, select *Chart of Accounts*.

3. Under the "Action" column, select *View Register*.

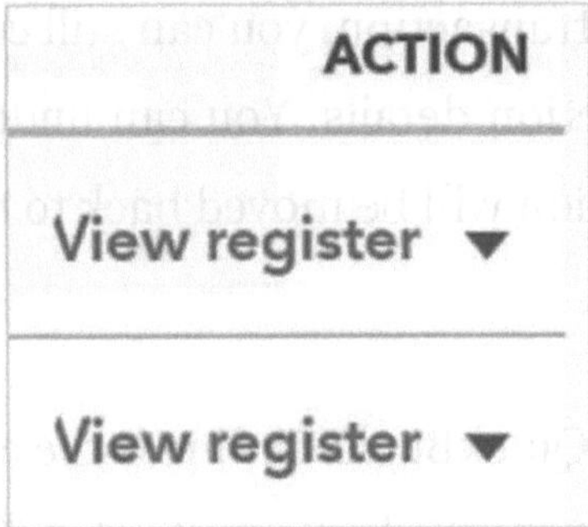

Registers work just like your checkbook. You can see/edit each transaction along with the account balance.

At the top of the register, you will find the account balance recorded at the bank/credit card company and the Account Balance in QuickBooks Online. These numbers often differ due to uncategorized transactions or the timing of the last import. Transactions are listed in order by date, starting with the most recent, although you can sort by any column by selecting the title name.

The register includes the following columns from left to right:

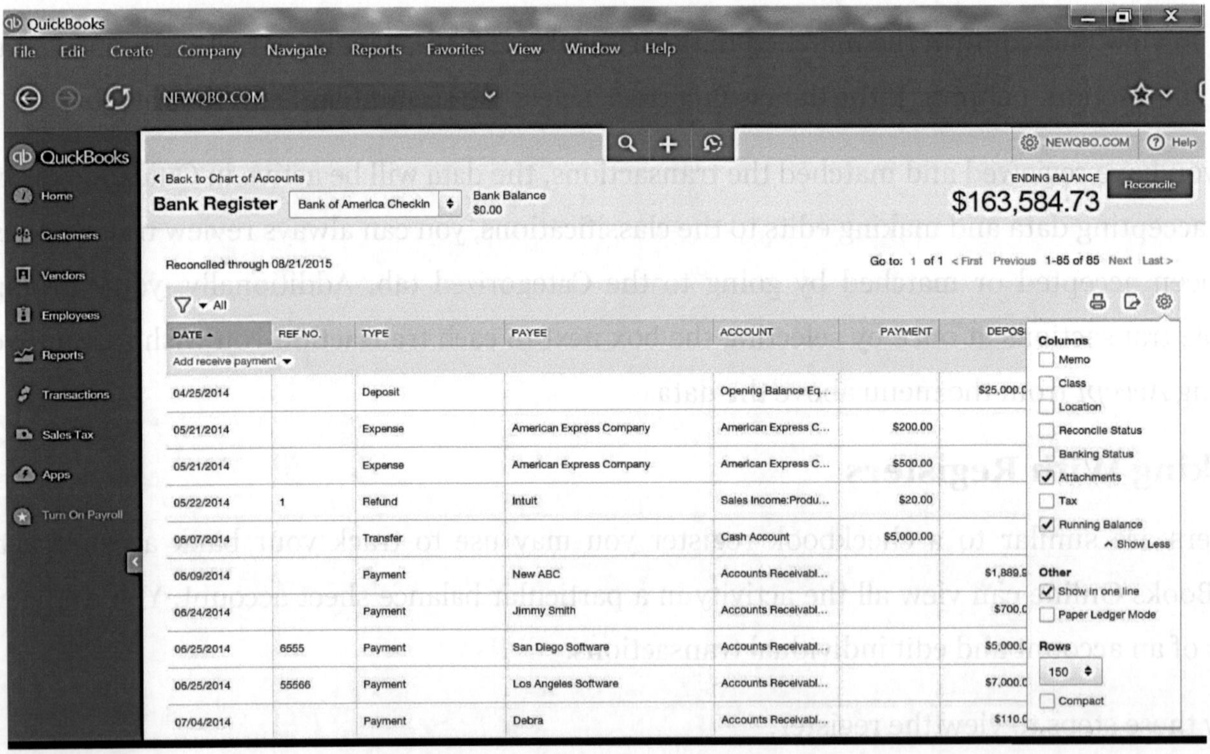

The register is a good place to review transactions and identify any issues. You can edit specific entries from the register and view the account balance.

- *Date*: the date the transaction took place
- *Ref No. Type*: the check number or invoice number and the type of transaction (deposit, check, payment, expense, credit card etc.).
- *Payee / Account*: the person who received or paid the funds and the account where the transaction was directed.
- *Memo*: the details written by the person inputting the transaction to describe the activity.
- *Payment*: the amount that came out of the account
- *Deposit*: the amount that went into the account
- *Check Mark*: this indicates if the transaction was imported via a bank feed
- *Balance*: the account balance at the time of the transaction.

Registers can also be used to add transactions manually to a particular account. In most cases, it's recommended that you import your bank data from your financial institution, but some accountants prefer to input the data manually.

Here is how to manually add transactions to the register:

1. Start by selecting the *Settings* icon (⚙).
2. Under the "Your Company" column, select *Chart of Accounts*.
3. Under the "Action" column on the right side of the screen, select *View Register*.
4. Select the *Settings* icon (⚙) on the register sheet (not the main settings icon).
5. Select *Paper Ledger Mode*. Once in the paper ledger mode, a new transaction input screen will appear at the bottom of the register.

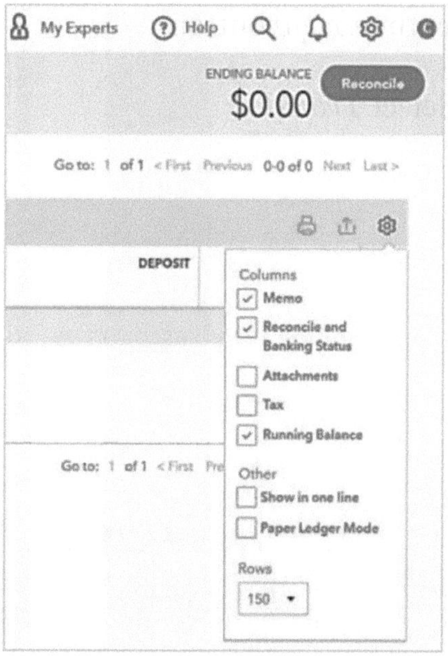

Select the columns you wish to be included in the register.

6. Select the type of transaction you wish to manually add from the drop-down box on the top of the transaction.
7. Add the transaction details, including the date, reference number, payee, account, memo, and amount.
8. Select *Save*.

Using this method, you can manually add transactions, including checks, deposits, sales receipts, received payments, bill payments, refunds, expenses, transfers, and journal entries.

Once done manually entering transactions, you can go back to the default screen by selecting the *Settings* icon (⚙) on the register sheet (not the main settings icon) and unchecking the "Paper Ledger Mode" box.

Bank Transfers

Transferring funds between your balance sheet accounts can be easily done in QuickBooks Online. Keeping an "emergency fund" in a savings account separate from your operating account is recommended by most business advisors. It's common to transfer money between these accounts as your business grows or as cash is needed to sustain business operations. Transferring between these accounts is a simple process in QuickBooks Online using the Transfer function.

Here is how to make a Transfer in QuickBooks Online:

1. From the **Dashboard**, Select the *+New* button.
2. Under the "Other" column, Select *Transfer*.

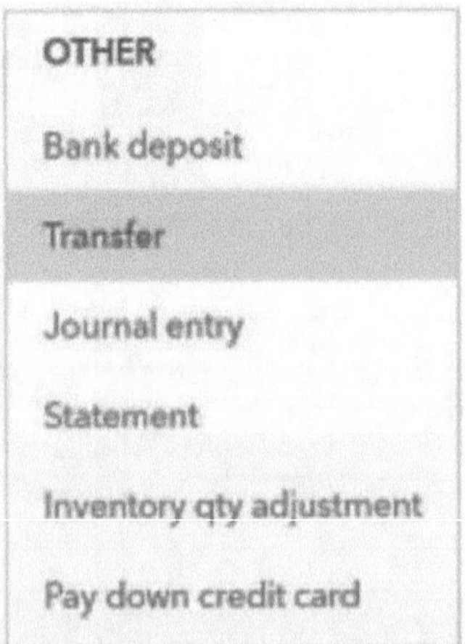

3. Select the account from where the funds are transferred "From" and "To" using the drop-down menus.
4. Input the amount of transfer.
5. Select the date of transfer.
6. Write a description in the "Memo" section.

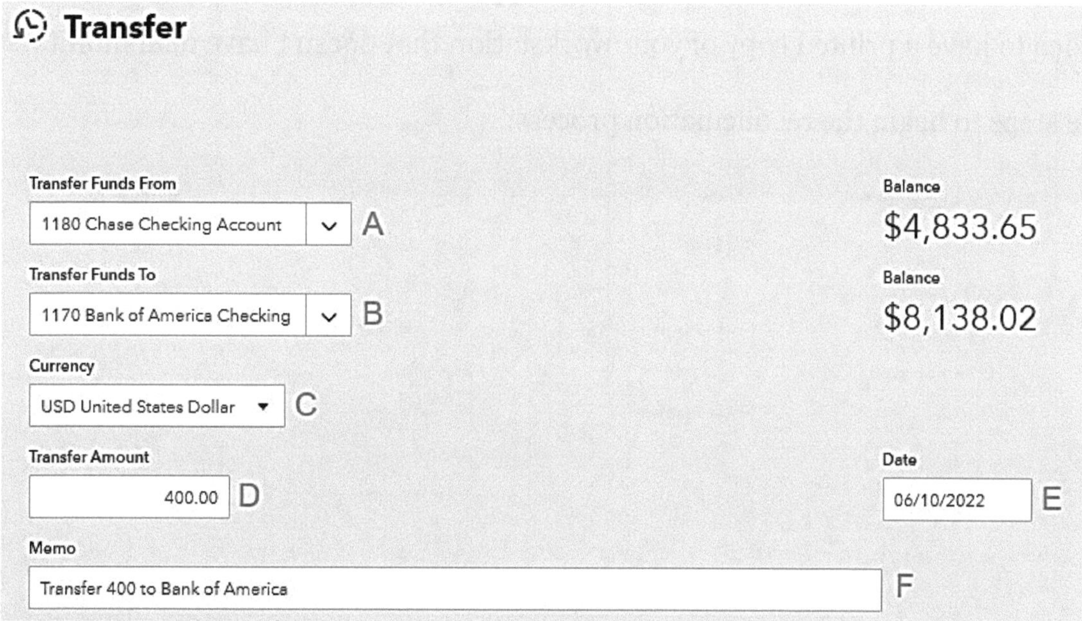

Using transfers is the correct way to move money between your business accounts.

7. Select Save and close.

As you can see, keeping up with bank transfers can be simple if done correctly. Next, let's look at bank reconciliations.

Bank Reconciliations

Once you have all your activity organized into QuickBooks Online, it's time to ensure you have everything properly recorded. The reconciliation process is often overlooked by business owners who self-prepare their financials. They either don't understand the importance of the reconciliation process, or they are unaware that it needs to be done at all. Either way, not reconciling is a big mistake.

The bank reconciliation aims to tie your bank statements to your financials to ensure they agree. Starting with your beginning bank balance, you will check off each deposit and expense made during the period, ending with your bank balance. For example, if your checking account had the following balances, the reconciliation would ensure all the activity was included in your books:

Beginning Balance	$11,589.23
Deposits	$5,889.78
Checks	($1,000.00)
Expenses	($2,399.66)
Ending Balance	$14,079.35

In this example, the bank balance started the period with $11,589.23 and ended with $14,079.35.

Before starting a reconciliation, you should have a copy of your bank statement on a separate screen. It's a good idea to have a printed copy of your workstation that doesn't have dual monitors.

Follow these steps to begin the reconciliation process:

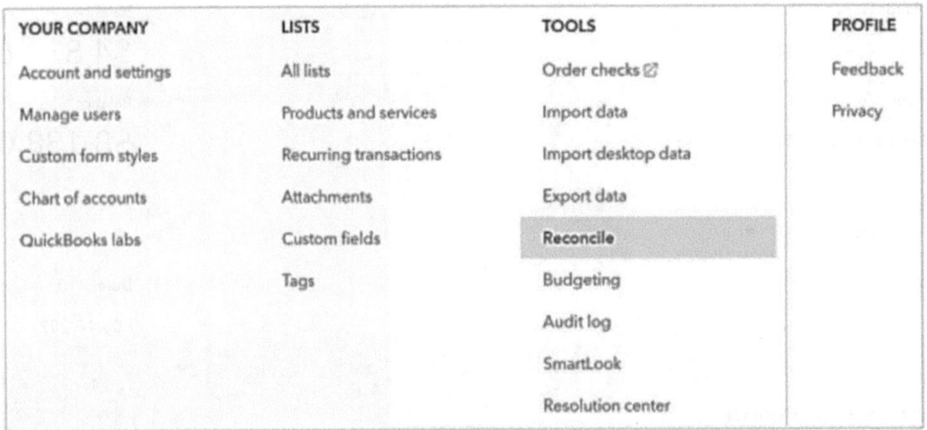

The reconciliation process ensures your books are accurate and all the activity from your bank account or credit card is included in your books.

1. Start by selecting the *Settings* icon (⚙) from the **Dashboard**.
2. Under the "Tools" column, select *Reconciliation.*
3. Under the *Account* drop-down menu, select the account you wish to reconcile.
4. Enter your *Ending Balance* and *Ending Date* from your bank statement.

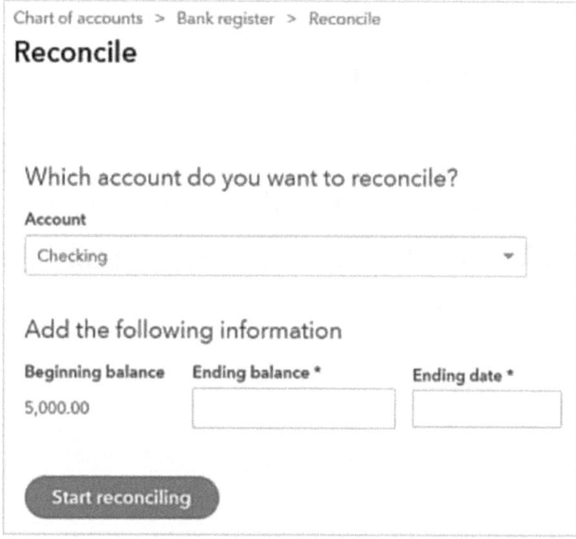

Select the account, ending balance, and date from your bank statement. The reconciliation process confirms that all deposits and expenses have been recorded in your books.

1. Select the Deposits tab and match your monthly deposits to the bank statement.
2. Select the Payments tab and match all your monthly expenses and checks to your bank statement.

Once the difference balance shows zero ($0.00), everything is balanced, and you are ready to reconcile.

3. Once all your activity has been selected for the month, the difference should be $0.00 with a green check mark.
4. Select *Finish Now*.

Each bank account and credit card reconciliation should be done monthly to ensure your books are accurate and all your activity has been properly recorded.

Reconciliations will often expose duplicate transactions or missing information. In this case, you will need to fix the issues by deleting a duplicate transaction or adding the missing activity. You can either manually adjust or enter the bank account register and input the change.

Chapter 6:

GST and BAS

Setting Up GST

The Instalment Activity Statement or Business Activity (BAS) lodging of your company early enough is a significant part of business operation in Australia. No one will be willing to pay FTL (Failure To Lodge) consequences plus other expenses when they have gotten to a point where there is tight cash flow. These expenses are the primary reason for the early BAS or IAS.

This feature is for people that have registered for GST. If you have not registered for GST, you do not need this feature because this setting, if tampered with, can permanently change things in your file.

When setting up a file for a new company, you must pay close attention to GST settings. Once the settings are complete as a part of the setup for the company, you cannot change them. You cannot change the GST period beginning, so make sure it is correct.

Setting Up Tax Centre For Clients

It is not hard; all you need to do is to follow the steps below.

1. From the navigation menu on the left hand, select the GST option.
2. Select Get Started.

When you select Get Started, your screen will look like the picture above. The picture above is the screen for Setting up BAS.

1. Choose the correct BAS, PAYG Instalments, and PAYG Withholding frequencies.

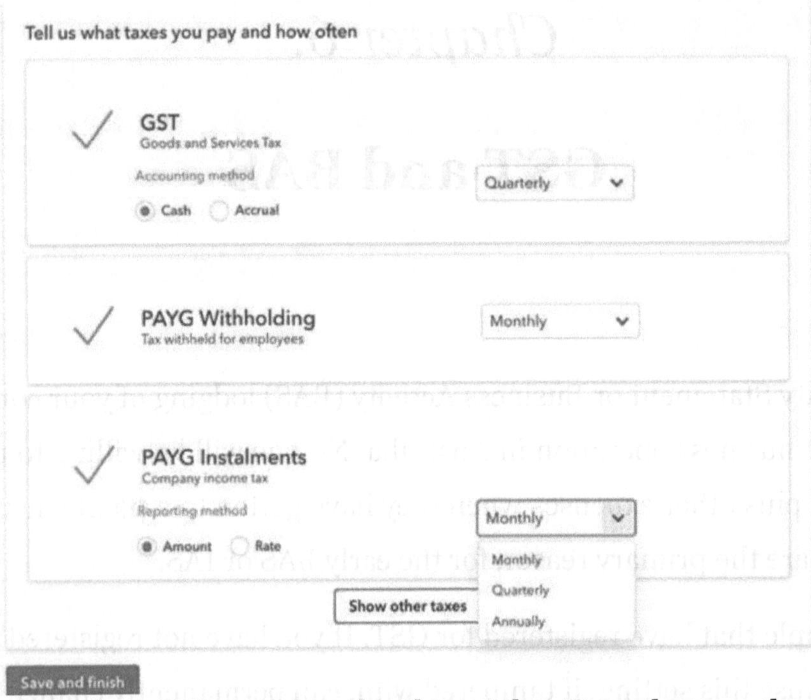

If you need other tax reporting options, select the Show Other Taxes button, then click to mark or tick the taxes that are relevant to you.

1. If you are sure, you have selected the relevant taxes, select Save and Finish.
2. Then click Done.

Chapter 7:

Staff and Payroll

Hiring employees is a big achievement in your business' growth. It's a sign of your business' success and stability. As a business owner, employees will allow you to delegate certain tasks and focus your time on the vision of your business.

Setting up and managing payroll can be a huge headache if not done correctly. Payroll must be prepared appropriately because paying employees, submitting taxes, and filing payroll reports can be time-consuming and tricky. Luckily, QuickBooks Online makes it manageable.

We will focus on payroll processing for United States-based companies. If you are operating in another country or hiring employees in other countries, you will want to check those countries' payroll processing methods to determine the correct filing procedures.

QuickBooks Online offers two payroll options: a Full-Service Payroll option and a do-it-yourself route called the Self-Service Payroll. The Full-Service Payroll option takes care of all the work for you, so we'll focus on the Self-Service Payroll option.

Preparing For Payroll – Documents & Decisions

First, let's clarify what's included in "payroll taxes", as this term includes multiple taxes calculated at different rates. Payroll taxes include the following:

- *Federal Income Tax Withholdings* – this amount is calculated based on your employee's W-4. Each employee will be different, as everyone's income and deductions are personal to their situation.
- *Social Security* – the current tax rate is 6.2% for the employee and 6.2% for the employer, for 12.4% on the first $142,800 income for the tax year 2021.
- *Medicare* – the current tax rate is 1.45% for the employee and 1.45% for the employer, for a total of 2.9% on all earned wages.
- *Federal Unemployment* – this is an employer's only tax and is 6% on the employee's first $7,000 of wages, for a maximum liability of $42 per employee.

State taxes will be different for each state, so it's recommended that you contact the state tax office to determine when and how to remit withholdings. You must register in the state where your employees are located to obtain a State Employer ID Number. You will need this to remit state withholdings and other payroll tax filings. Seven states do not charge a state income tax: Alaska, Florida, Nevada, New Hampshire, South Dakota, Tennessee, Texas, Washington, and Wyoming. These states may not require additional filings but check with your state to be sure. Employers must generally withhold taxes in the states where employees perform their work.

You often hear of professional sports athletes having to file in multiple states based on where they played during the season. This is because state tax is based on where the work is performed. If you have employees traveling to multiple states, you may generate a filing requirement in those states.

Before we can set up payroll information in QuickBooks Online, you will need to document your new employee's personal information and decide how you will run payroll. On your new employee's first day, you will have them fill out the following documents needed to run payroll:

- *W-4 Employee's Withholding Certificate (IRS)* – this form provides the employee's address, social security number, income tax filing status, and the information needed to determine the withholdings on their paycheck.
- *State withholding forms* – most states have a state income tax (excluding nine states), and each state has a withholding form similar to the W-4 that will allow you to calculate its state withholding amount in QuickBooks Online.
- *I-9 Employment Eligibility Verification* – this form confirms that the employee is eligible to work in the United States.
- *Two forms of government-issued ID* –would include a driver's license, social security card, or other government-issued ID.
- *Direct deposit authorization form* – request your employee's account type, bank routing number, account number, and percentage to be deposited into the account. Each employee can elect to split each deposit amount into two bank accounts.

These documents should be kept in your employee's file.

In addition to your new employee's set-up documents, you will need to know the following information or make the following decisions:

- *Hire Date* – this is the first day of employment with your company. This should be included in the offer letter to your employee. The hire date is used to calculate accrued vacation, holiday pay, and sick pay.
- *Pay Rate or Salary* is the established hourly wage, salary, or commission agreed upon in the initial offer letter.
- *Frequency* – QuickBooks Online allows you to set your employees' frequency and pay schedule. Based on your industry, the typical payroll cycle is either weekly, biweekly, semi-monthly, or monthly.

- *Payment Method* – the method you will use to pay your employee. This could be a paper check or direct deposit.
- *Benefits* – common benefits include retirement benefits (401k, SIMPLE, SEP) and health insurance. You will need to know the employee's portion of contribution and your (the employer's) match or paid portion. Often these benefits take 60-90 days from the hire date to become effective.
- *Other adjustments* could include child support, employee advances, or industry-specific adjustments.

Activating Payroll In Quickbooks Online

Now that you have a basic understanding of payroll taxes, decided when and how to make payroll, and have all the essential employee documents, it's time to activate payroll in QuickBooks Online. QuickBooks Online uses a wizard to help activate and set up your initial payroll accounts and employees.

Follow these steps to activate payroll in QuickBooks Online:

1. From the **Dashboard**, select *Payroll* from the left-hand menu.
2. Select Get Started.

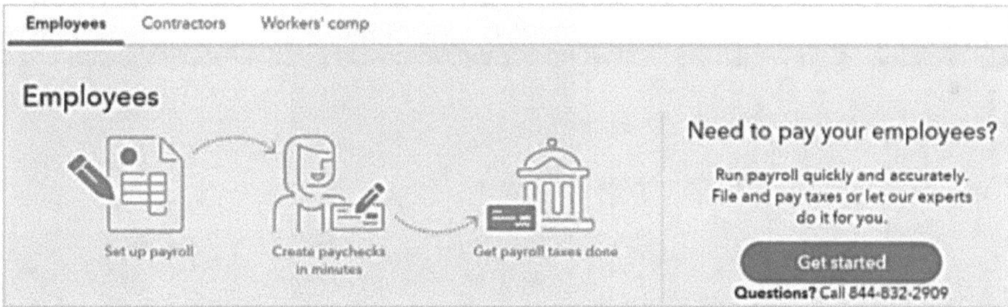

3. Select either the *QuickBooks Self-Service Payroll* or the *QuickBooks Full-Service Payroll.* We will use self-service in this book since the full-service option performs all these tasks for you.

The QuickBooks Online Wizard will ask if you have had payroll during the year before activating QuickBooks Online payroll. If you used another payroll service or QB Desktop, you would want to properly run the historical data to set up QuickBooks Online Payroll. QuickBooks Online will need this information to prepare your W-2s and 1099s for contractors accurately.

Once the account is activated, you can view the employee dashboard. This is where you can run payroll, add employees, add, and review benefits, file taxes, and adjust your company preferences.

Company Payroll Preferences

As you have seen in other sections of QuickBooks Online, setting up your preferences is key to successfully working in QuickBooks Online. The preferences allow you to establish your various payroll settings.

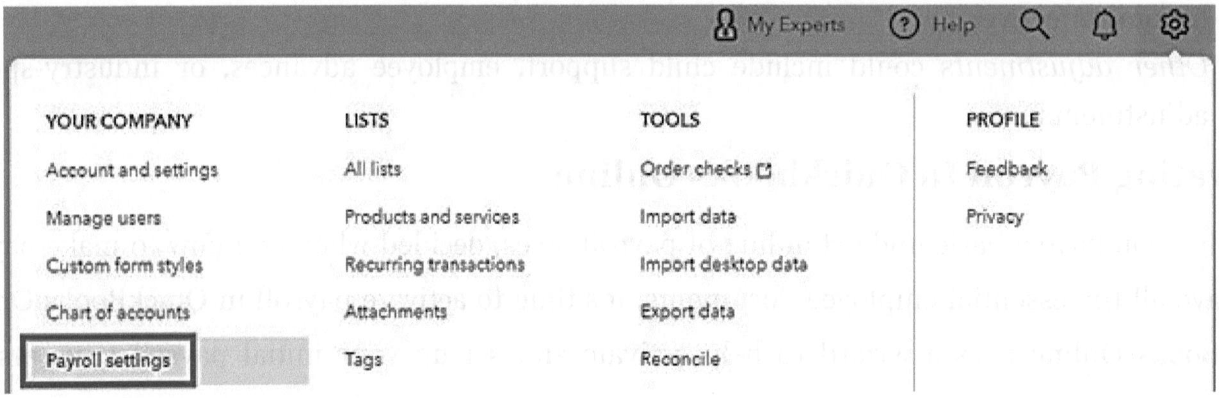

To access your payroll preferences, head to the *Settings* icon (⚙)and select *Payroll Settings* under the "Your Company" column. Under each tab, select *Edit* ✎ to edit each section. You should go through each section and add the required information. The "General Tax" section will confirm your company's legal name, entity status, and filing address.

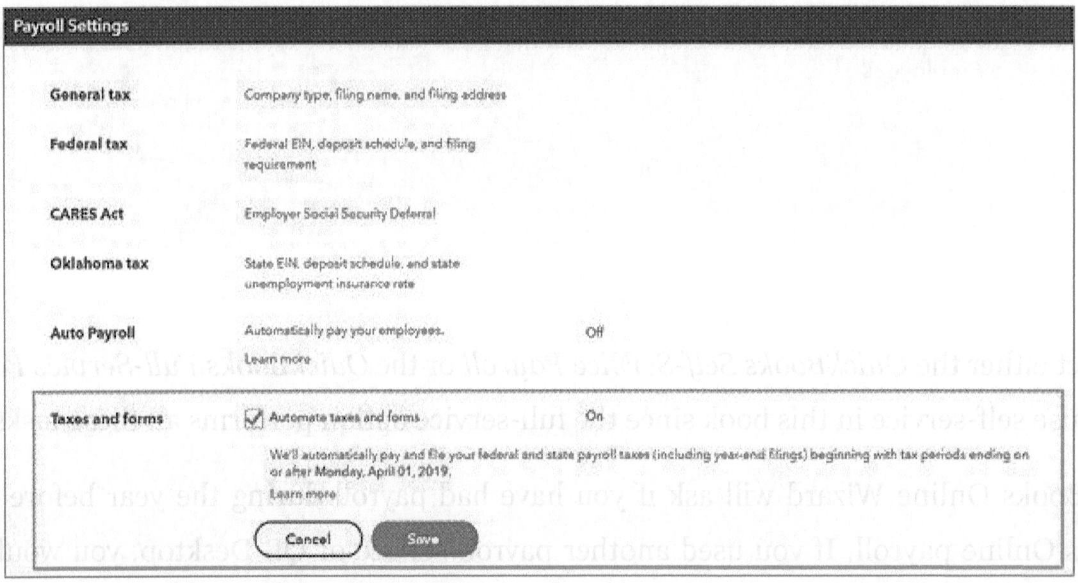

It's important to ensure this information ties to your formation documents because it will be included in your tax filings.

Add An Employee

QuickBooks Online will prompt you to set up employees as part of the activation process, but you can also manually add employees as your business grows.

Follow these steps to set up an employee in QuickBooks Online:

1. From the **Dashboard**, select *Payroll* from the left-hand menu.
2. Select Employees.

3. From the Employees home screen, select *Add an employee.*
4. Enter your new employee's personal information, including their name, address, social security number, hire date, and email address.

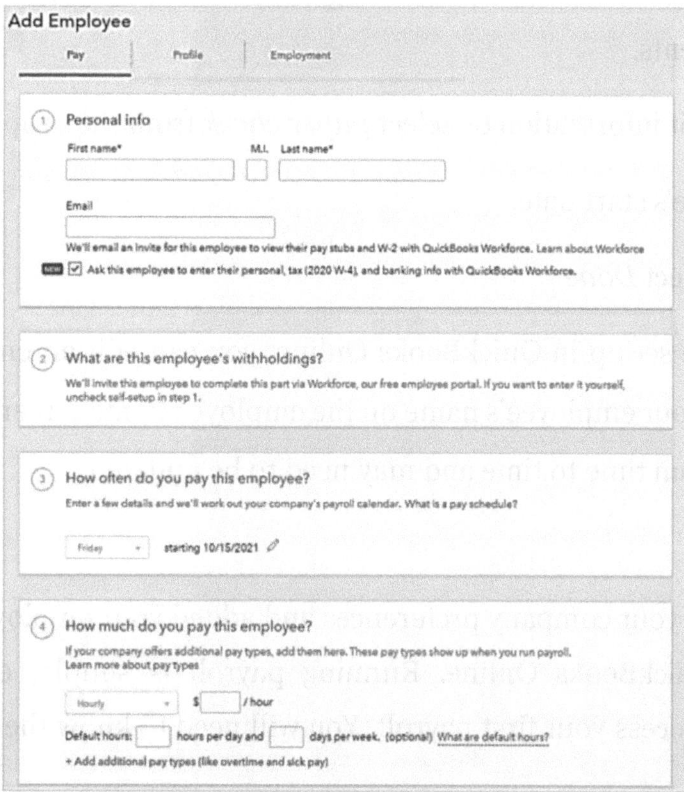

Use the forms your employee filled out to input these screens.

5. Enter the employee's W-4 payroll tax withholding information and hourly pay rate or salary.

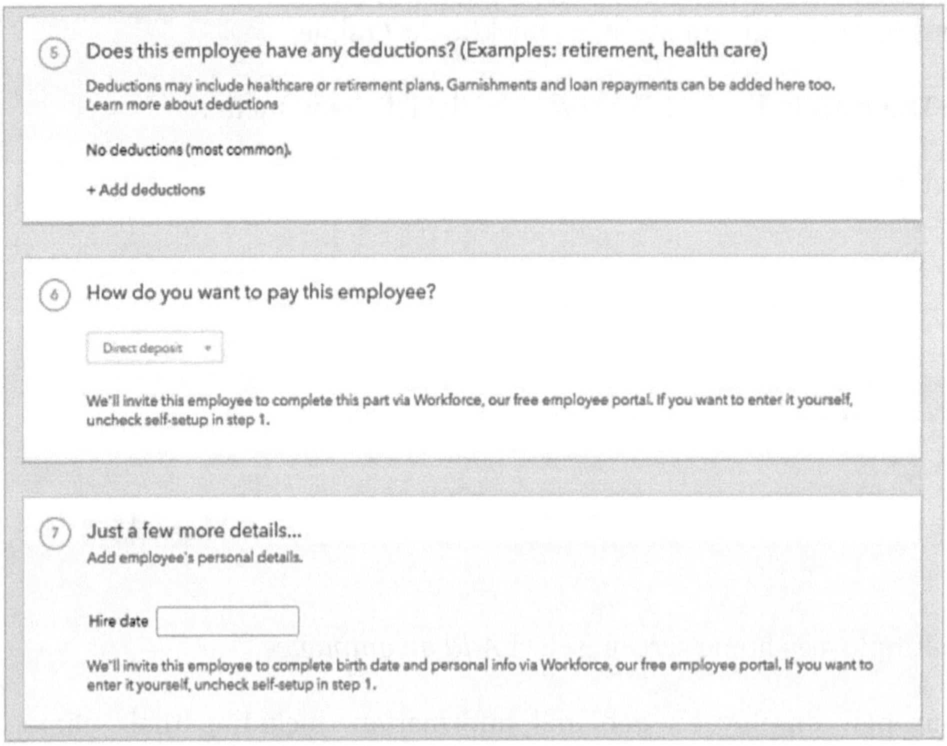

6. Enter the employee's deductions, including health care, retirement contributions or child support garnishments.
7. Enter direct deposit information or select *paper check* from the drop-down menu.
8. Enter the employee's start date.
9. Once complete, select *Done.*

Once your employees are set up in QuickBooks Online, you can edit an employee's information by selecting *Edit* ✎ next to your employee's name on the employee home screen. Employees may change their W-4 information from time to time and may need to be updated.

Running Payroll

Now that you have set up your company preferences and added your employees, it's time to run your first payroll cycle in QuickBooks Online. Running payroll is simple; ensure you have all the information needed to process your first payroll. You will need to know the dates for the pay period, your employee's hours for the pay period, their rates or salary, and how your employee' will be paid (direct deposit or checks).

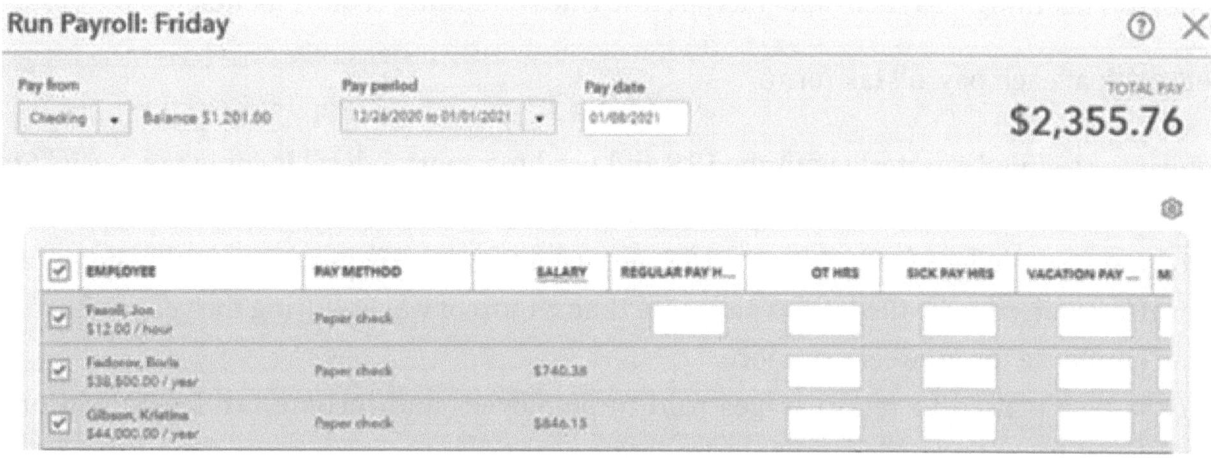

1. From the **Dashboard**, select the *+New* button, then select *Payroll* under the "Employee" column.

2. Select the bank account you used to set up your payroll. (Note: changing this account will not change the account from which the funds are withdrawn.)

3. Confirm the pay period and that the pay date is accurate.

4. Review/enter your employee's hours and payment amount. You can change the payment method for each employee on this screen.

5. Once you have completed entering the payroll information, select *Preview Payroll.*

6. Review each employee's total pay, taxes, and net pay. Once you are satisfied that the payroll cycle is accurate, select *Submit Payroll.*

7. Print checks and pay stubs for each employee.

Once direct-deposited checks have been submitted, you will have a short window to make corrections. From the home page, under related activities, select *View Paycheck List*. Check the status, and if your payroll has not yet been processed, you can delete the paychecks and start over. If the payroll cycle has already been processed, you will need to contact QuickBooks Online to see if the payroll cycle can be cancelled.

Paying And Filing Payroll Taxes

Both federal and state governments require the filing of payroll tax returns. QuickBooks Online will automatically submit your payroll taxes and tax returns unless you opt-out and choose to complete these tasks manually. Each state has different filing requirements, so it's recommended that you research your state's filing requirements and file them accordingly. This book will focus on your federal payroll tax filings, as each state has specific rules and filing requirements.

First, let's look at each payroll tax form:

- *Form 941* – filed quarterly with the IRS and used to report federal income tax, Social Security tax, and Medicare tax withheld from employees' paychecks.
- *Form 940* – filed annually with the IRS and used to report Federal Unemployment Tax. This form is required to be filed if you pay more than $1500 of wages during the year or have at least one employee for 20 weeks or more.
- *Form W-2* – used to report wages paid to employees and income taxes withheld on those wages. W-2's must be filed annually by January 31st.
- *Form 1099 NEC* – This new tax form for 2020 is used to pay independent contractors. This form must be issued to contractors who paid more than $600 in a tax year. It also must be filed by January 31st.

As an employer, you must regularly remit payroll tax withholdings and payroll taxes. This is one of the most important responsibilities of an employer. Remember that you are submitting money that you withheld from your employees, so this is technically their money. The remittance schedule will vary depending on your amount of payroll, but taxes are typically required to be submitted semi-weekly or monthly.

QuickBooks Online does a great job reminding you when payments need to be made and when tax forms need to be submitted. Although QuickBooks Online tracks these due dates, it's good practice to put all your tax deadlines on your calendar at the beginning of the year to ensure you don't overlook a due date.

QuickBooks Online will also automatically make your federal and state tax payments using your linked account when you set up your payroll. There is an option to opt-out of the automatic payments and make your payments yourself, though this is not recommended unless you have a background in payroll and understand all the payment and filing deadlines.

You can make federal and state tax payments through QuickBooks Online, which will be automatically withdrawn from your selected bank account. Processing times will vary depending on the taxing authority, but most taxing agencies take two business days to transfer and accept payment.

Here is how to manually schedule a tax payment through QuickBooks Online:

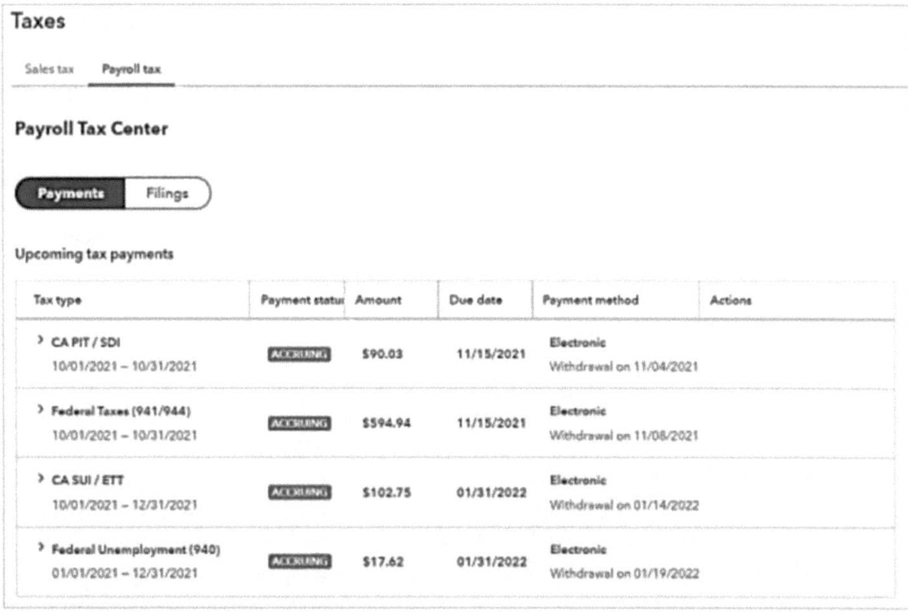

1. From the **Dashboard**, select *Taxes* on the left-hand menu, then select *Payroll Tax.*
2. Select *Payments* from the toggle.
3. Select *Pay Taxes* under the "Tax" section you wish to pay, then select *Create Payment.*
4. Select *E-pay* and choose the date to pay taxes. Select *Approve* and *Done.*

QuickBooks Online will now automatically make your tax filings unless, similarly to payments, you opt-out and choose to file your taxes manually. Again, this is not recommended if you do not have the proper experience.

Here is how to manually file payroll tax reports:

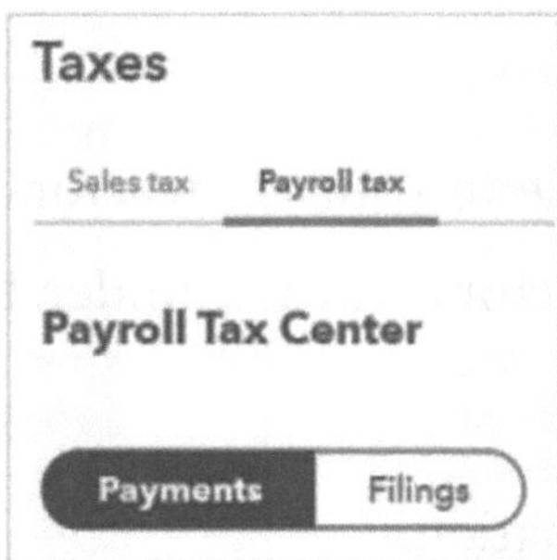

1. From the **Dashboard**, select *Taxes* on the left-hand menu, then select *Payroll Tax.*
2. Select *Filings.*
3. Select the tax form you wish to submit.

4. Review the information and confirm the inputs. Once ready, select *Submit.*

Again, payroll taxes and filings are completed automatically by QuickBooks Online but can be completed manually if you opt out.

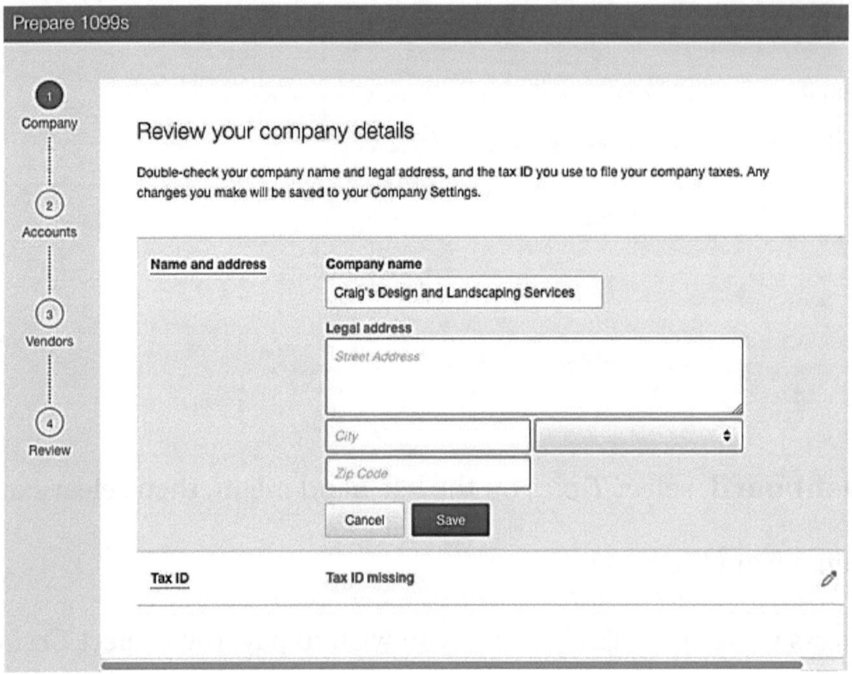

1. Select Payroll from the **dashboard** on the left-hand menu then selects *Contractors.*
2. Select Prepare 1099s
3. Select the green *Let's get started* button.
4. Review your company's information; ensure your business name, address, EIN, and phone number are accurate.
5. Select the type of payments made to your contractors during the year (1099-MISC or 1099-NEC). Most independent contractors will fall under the "non-employee compensation" box 1099-NEC.
6. Confirm your contractor's information.
7. Review the payments and personal information once you are satisfied that all contractors have been included and the amounts are accurate, select *E-File for me*, and print copies to keep in your files.

QuickBooks Online offers two options to file 1099s. The first option is to e-file your 1099s, including an emailed delivery of the 1099s to your contractors and a mailed hard copy. The second option is to have Intuit send you a printed kit to mail yourself. This is more expensive, but some businesses prefer to mail the copies themselves.

Chapter 8:
Inventory

Enabling Inventory In Quickbooks

Inventory tracking enables you always to know how much stock is on hand. Using the accounting software QuickBooks, you may monitor your inventory in real-time. This functionality is available in QuickBooks but is not immediately active when the software is installed. In actuality, you must activate the inventory option in QuickBooks. QuickBooks Enterprise, Premier, and Pro provide inventory tracking as an optional feature.

- Log in to QuickBooks using your administrator credentials. The administrator can only activate the inventory.
- To access the "Edit" menu, click on it. Once the menu has opened, select "Preferences." This launches the Options window.
- Select Items & Inventory" in the list of editable settings. Navigate to the "Company Preferences" section from there.
- Mark the box next to "Inventories and purchase orders are active." Select the box by clicking on it.
- Click the "OK" button to save your modifications. This enables inventory management in QuickBooks.

How To Create New Inventory Part Items

You can add inventory and non-inventory items for tracking purposes to QuickBooks. Inventory items are those your company has in stock; for instance, if you own an electronics store, you may track the quantity of a certain television model. Items that are not in stock include those that are specifically ordered or drop-shipped directly to the consumer. Before creating inventory parts in QuickBooks, you must enable inventory tracking; however, you can create non-inventory parts without modifying the QuickBooks settings.

- Open QuickBooks
- Afterwards, select "Preferences" from the "Edit" menu.
- Select the "Company Preferences" tab after clicking the "Items & Inventory" button.
- Check the "Inventory and purchase orders are active" box to enable inventory tracking. Select "OK"

- Select "Items & Services" on the Home pane, then click "Item," followed by "New."
- Choose "Inventory Part" from the drop-down option labeled Type.
- Input the inventory item's name in the "Item Name/Number" text box. Click the "Income Account" drop-down menu and choose the account you'd like to use to track income from this inventory item.
- Select the "OK" option to create the inventory section after filling in the remaining required fields.

How To Create A Purchase Order

1. If you have not done so already, activate purchase orders:

- Under Edit, select **Preferences.**
- Choose **Items & Inventory**, followed by the tab labeled **Company Preferences**.
- Ensure the Inventory and purchase orders are active box, then click **OK.**

2. **Click** Create Purchase Orders within **the Vendors menu.**
3. Select the vendor for whom you would want to place a purchase order from the Vendor dropdown menu. Additionally, you can select **Add New** to add a new vendor.
4. Fill out the remaining sections and add the things you wish to purchase.
5. Choose **Save** and Close.

Hint: Purchase orders are an integral component of the Accounts Payable (A/P) process.

How To Create Purchase Order Reports

You must generate two reports to compare the transactions and balances. This is how:

- **Select the** Reports button.
- **Select** Customized Reports.
- **Choose** Transaction Detail
- Click the button labeled **Customize Report.**
- Update the report date in the Display tab.
- On the same page, in the Columns section, click **Paid.**
- Select the Filter tab.
- In the Filter section, select Either from the options under Posting Status.
- Select **Transaction Type** from the Filters menu, and then select **Purchase Order** from the drop-down menu.
- Click **Accept.**
- In the **Total By drop-down**, select vendor.

This report will display received or billed purchase orders. Use the Open Purchase Orders by Job page to view open purchase orders. Follow the below steps:

- **Select the** Reports button.
- **Select** Purchases
- **Select** Open Purchase Orders by job
- Click the button labeled **Customize Report.**
- Select the Display tab.
- Select Debit and Credit in the Columns section.
- Click **Accept.**

How To Receive Inventory With A Bill

We can transform the PO into a bill each time you get an item from a purchase order (PO). The item's quantity will be added to the inventory (Products and Services) list. This is how;

- Select the "+New" button.
- Beneath Vendor, select **Bill.**
- Click the drop-down arrow next to Vendor and select the vendor's name.
- All existing purchase orders will be displayed on the left. Select the appropriate PO, then click **Add.**
- Click **Save** and close when finished.

If you received the goods without a receipt, we can still alter the quantity and not record a transaction. In other words, we can match your inventory. I'll guide you on how:

- Select the "+New" button.
- **In the Other column, choose** Inventory quantity adjustment.
- Enter the date of the adjustment and select the items to amend.
- Click **Save** and then Exit.

Once the inventory modification is saved, QuickBooks automatically records the corresponding inventory account adjustments.

How To Enter Bills

After receiving a bill from a vendor, record it as follows:

- First and foremost, choose + **New**.
- Afterwards, choose Bill.
- Choose a vendor from the drop-down menu labeled **Vendor.**

- Specify the bill's terms from the drop-down menu labeled Terms. This is when your vendor anticipates receiving payment.
- Input the Due date, Bill date, and Bill number exactly as they appear on the bill.
- Input the details of the invoice in the Category details box. Select the cost account you use to track spending transactions from the Category selection. Enter a description, then. To itemize the bill, you can specify individual products and services in the Item details area.
- Enter the Amount with tax.
- Choose the Billable checkbox and put the customer's name in the Customer field if you intend to bill a customer for the spending. Learn more about chargeable expenses.
- When finished, select **Save** and Exit.

You may also choose locations from the Location drop-down menu if you have many workplaces or business divisions.

Track and pay bills

If you don't know how to pay bills in QuickBooks Online, entering your bills won't do you any good. Thankfully, the procedure is, once again, rather basic.

With QuickBooks Online, you may pay your vendors directly from your bank account by direct deposit or a paper check for free. You can also use a debit card or a credit card. Regardless of your preferred payment method, you will follow these steps to pay invoices in QuickBooks Online.

- Select the "Pay Bills" window.

There are two locations on your Dashboard where the "Pay Bills" link can be found. The first location is in the shortcuts menu and instructions for entering a bill.

The second method for initiating bill payment is to click the "New" button at the top of the page. You will next locate "Pay Bills" under the "Vendors" menu.

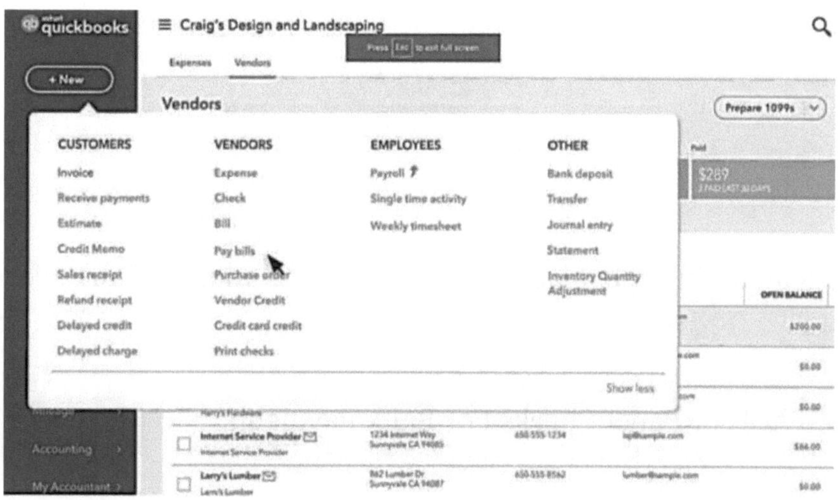

- Choose Your Bill

Locate the bill that you wish to pay among your list of bills. Click the left checkbox and choose "Online payment scheduling."

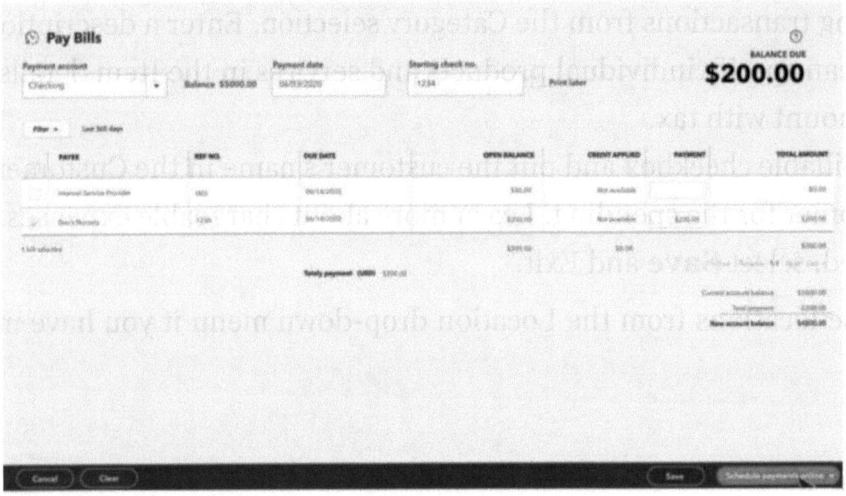

- Select Your Payment Method

Next, you must select your payment method. Payments made via bank account (including paper checks) and debit card are free. However, the credit card processing cost is 2.9% plus $0.25 for each transaction.

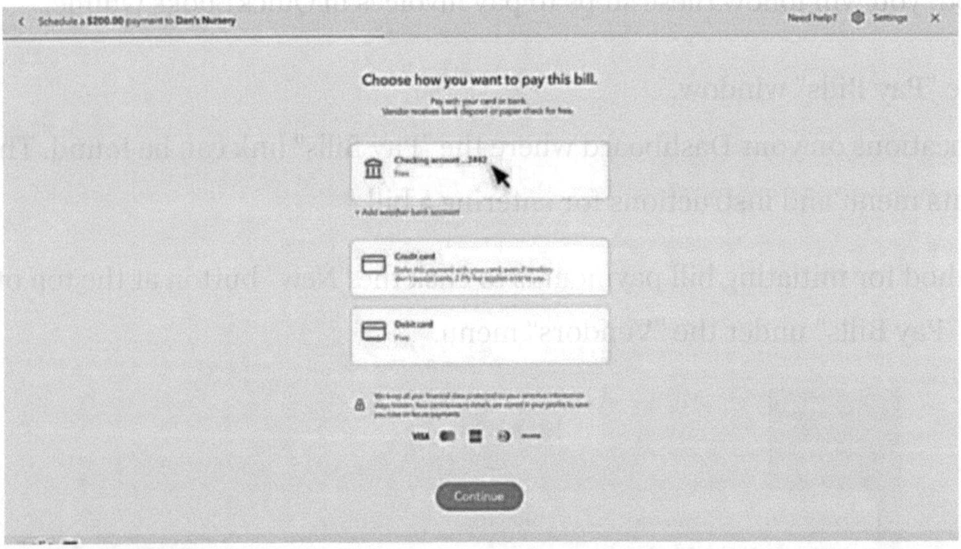

If you wish to pay with an unlinked bank account, select "Add another bank account" and follow the instructions.

- Decide Between ACH or Paper Checks For Bank Payments

If you opt to pay bills directly from your bank account in QuickBooks Online, you will be prompted with an additional screen where you can choose between direct deposit and a physical check.

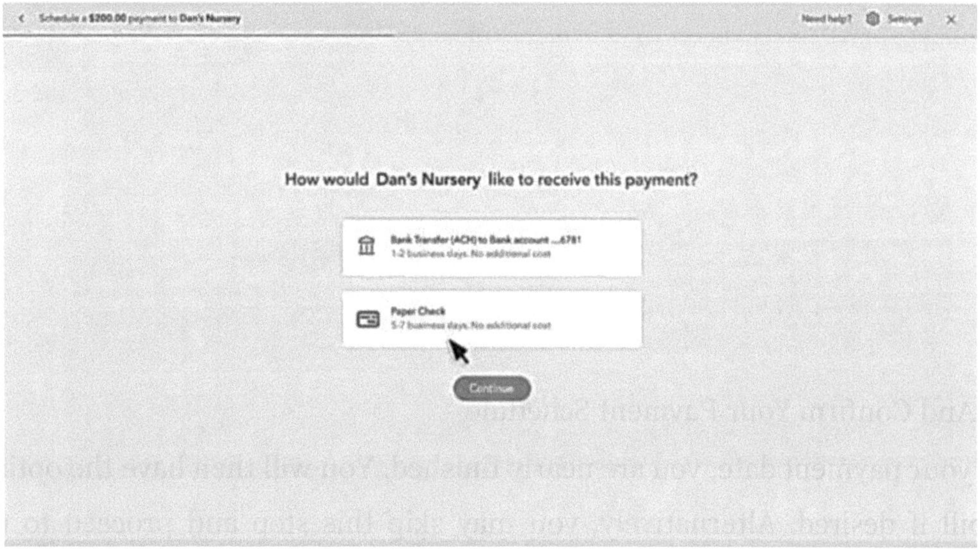

You can still send a paper check (if you or your vendor prefer this method) even if you plan payments online. Like bank bill pay services, QuickBooks handles everything for you, including printing and mailing the check.

Whether you choose ACH or a paper check does not affect the price. Each option is free. However, paper checks normally arrive within 5 to 7 business days, whereas bank transfers typically arrive within 1 to 2 business days.

- Select Your Payment Date

Next, a calendar will appear for you to select the date you would like your payment to be processed. Remember that this is the intended payment date, although it will arrive later. At the bottom of the scheduling calendar, the approximate arrival time of your bill will be displayed.

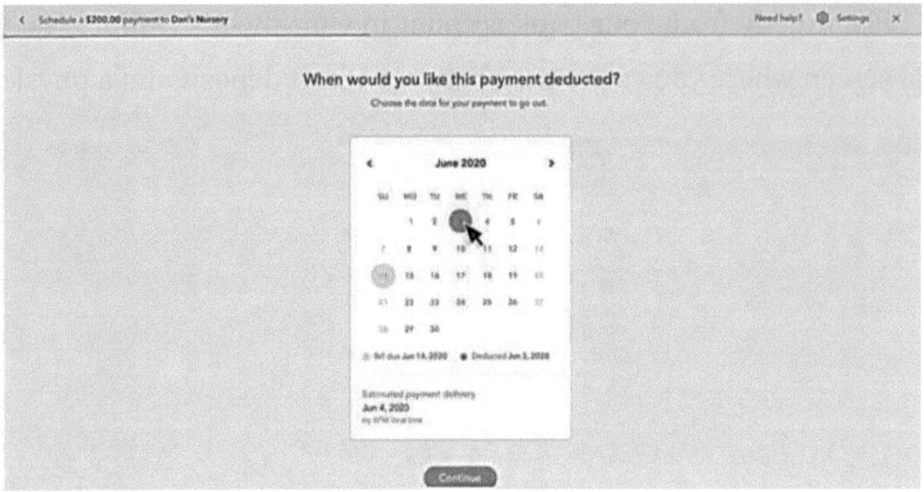

- Review And Confirm Your Payment Schedule

After selecting your payment date, you are nearly finished. You will then have the option to include a note to your bill if desired. Alternatively, you may skip this step and proceed to the "Review & Confirm" screen.

Check your bill payment's final details to ensure everything is in order. If so, you can then click "Confirm and Schedule Payment."

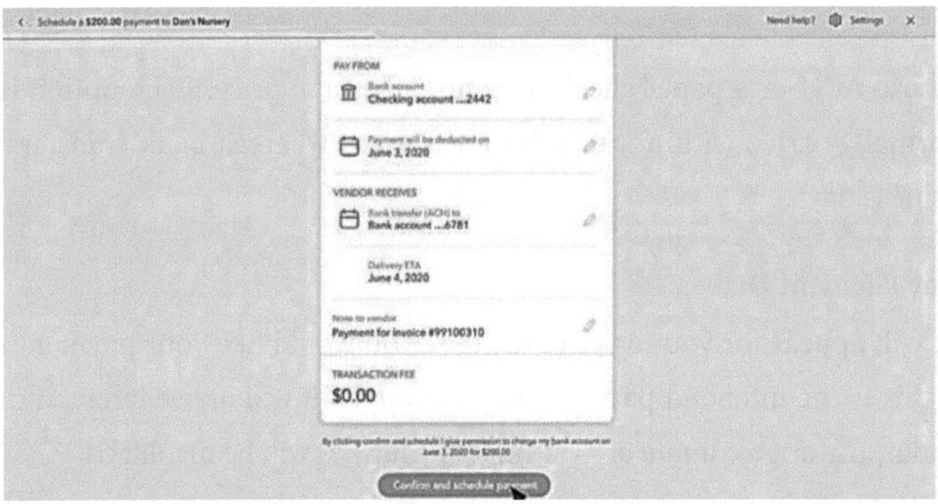

You have successfully scheduled your first bill payment in QuickBooks Online.

- Document your Bank Transaction

Your job is not yet complete. After the transaction is complete, the bank payment is matched with your bill as the final step. To accomplish this, you must navigate to "Bank Transactions."

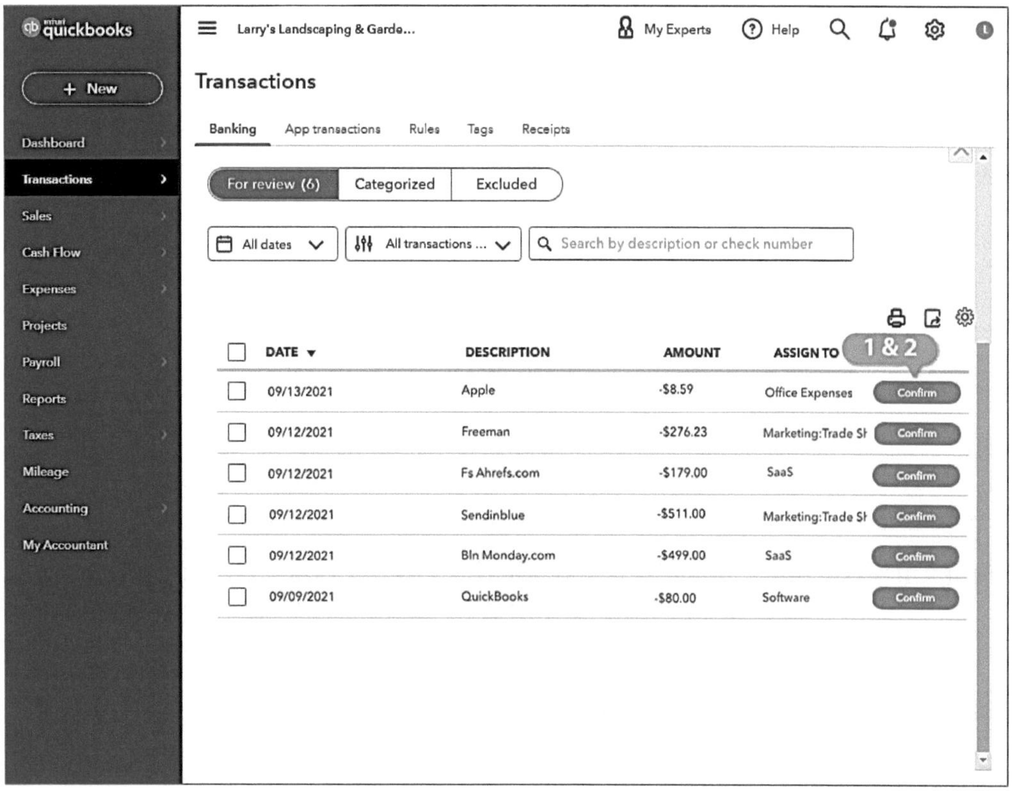

You'll see a list of all the transactions downloaded from your bank by QuickBooks. If one of your transactions is the same amount as a recent bill, QuickBooks may identify a probable matching record and highlight this in a green book.

You only need to select "Match" from the "Action" tab on the right.

And that concludes it! You have just finished all the QuickBooks Online bill entry and payment processes.

How To Create An Item Receipt

To produce an item receipt in QuickBooks Desktop, you must add the relevant bills to your inventory. This allows you to record the amount due for the item receipt conveniently. To enter the bill for the item receipt, select Enter Bills against Inventory from the Homepage. When you access the Select Item Receipt screen, you may choose the vendor, enter the correct date for the invoice, select the item receipt, and save details.

In QuickBooks Desktop, creating invoices against inventory is a standard A/P process. It is encouraged to review the list of vendor-related workflows and transactions.

- To access the "Home" screen in "QuickBooks Desktop," navigate to the "Home" screen.
- Then, select the option to "Enter Bills against Inventory."
- In the "Select Item Receipt" screen, choose the vendor's name from the "Vendor" drop-down menu.
- If the original inventory date is used, place a checkbox in the "Use Item receipt date for the bill date" box.
- Click on "Item Receipt" at this time. If multiple item receipts exist, ensure that each bill is converted separately.
- Select the OK button. This turns your "Item Receipt" into an invoice.

After completing these procedures, you can proceed with bill payment. Thus, you may quickly create the item receipt against the inventory and pay the charge.

If you have previously recorded the item receipt, you can create an item receipt in QuickBooks Desktop by following these steps:

- Select the "Vendors" button.
- Afterwards, select "Enter Bill for Received Items". This will open a window titled "Select Item Receipt."
- Now, select the vendor using the drop-down menu labeled "Vendor."
- QuickBooks will display a list of item receipts from the chosen vendors (Merge Vendors in QuickBooks). Choose the "Item Receipt" that corresponds to your bill.
- Select the OK button.
- When the "Enter Bills" window opens, QuickBooks will automatically enter the details from the item receipt into the text area.
- If the information entered by QuickBooks is incorrect, you can enter the "Date," "Bill Due," and "Amount Due" boxes manually.
- Using the "Conditions" drop-down box, you can examine payment terms and reference numbers to determine the vendor's reference number.
- Add the memo description, if desired, in the "Memo" box.
- Now, click the "Expenses" tab so that you can review the expenses represented by your bill.
- Once complete, describe the items on the "Items" tab.
- You can click "Save & Close" or "Save & New" to save further bill and item receipt information.

If the item receipt has already been recorded in QuickBooks Desktop, you can enter the bills in this manner. Make sure that each field contains the correct information.

Create Sales Receipt And Deposit

Do you provide products or services to customers and receive immediate payment? Find out how to generate QuickBooks sales receipts.

- Open Sales Receipt. Under Customers on the **Plus Sign Menu**, select Sales Receipt.

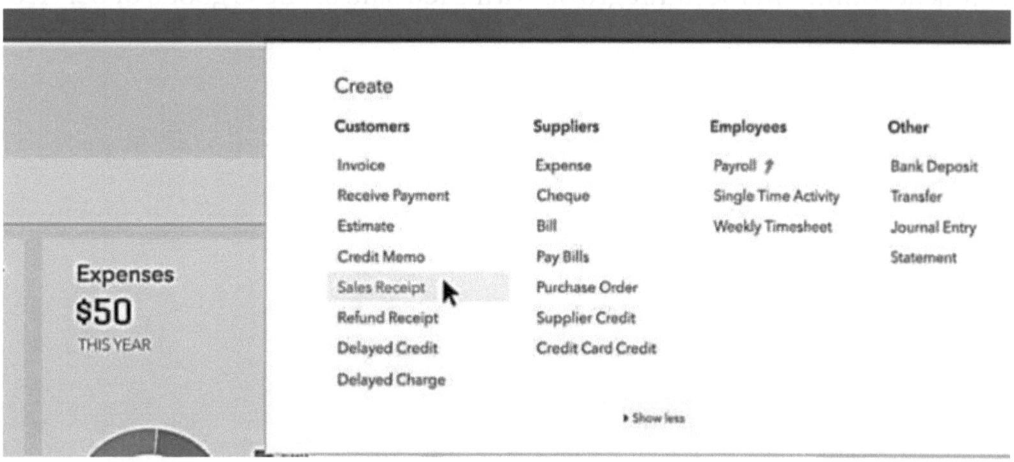

- Enter the Name of the Customer. Enter the customer's name who is paying you. If the customer is new, click Save.

You can simply name them with a generic "Internet Sales."

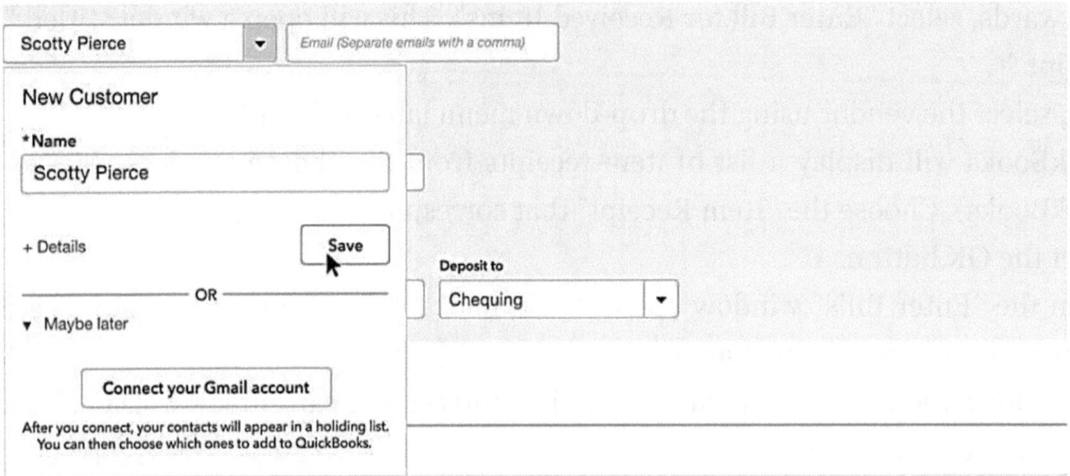

- Enter Goods and Services

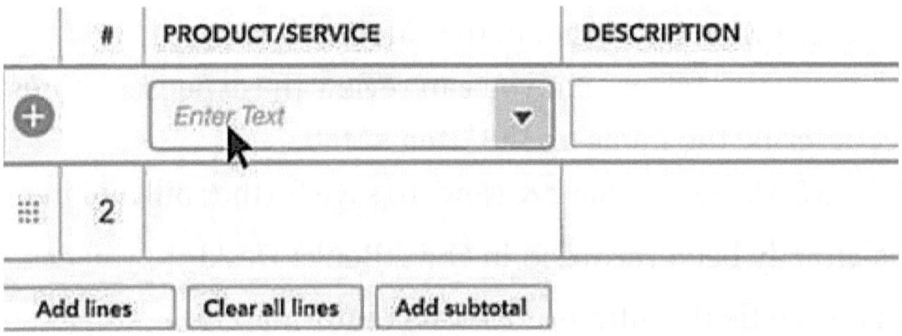

Enter the new product or service and click the Add button. Then, insert details regarding this product or service.

- Select a Revenue or Income Account

Select the Income Account inside the Product or Service Information pane. This is an accounting account, not a bank account. This account grows with each sale of these goods or services. Select Save.

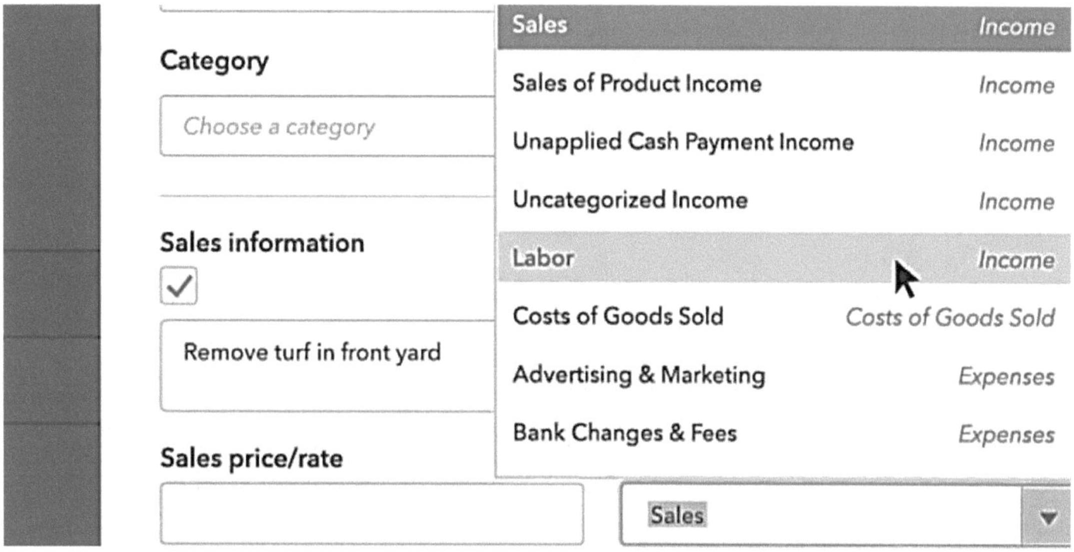

- Enter Payment Information

Input the Payment Method used by the consumer to pay you. In the Reference No. field, enter the cheque number if the payment was made by check.

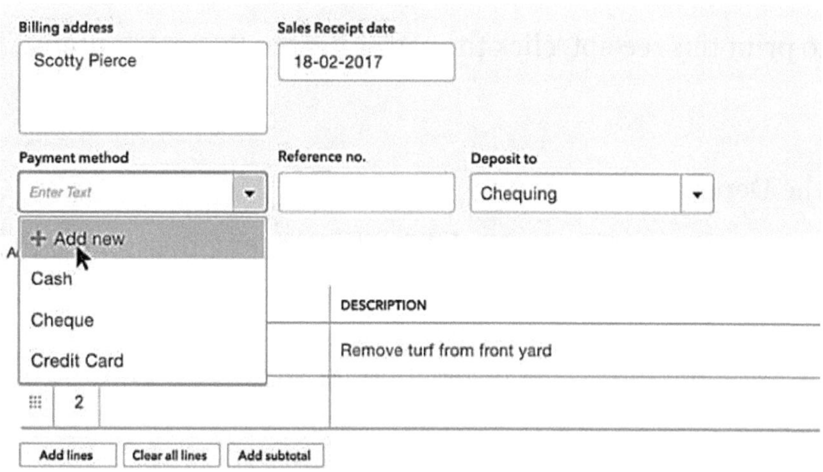

- Select Bank Account

Choose the bank account you placed money into under Deposit To. If you are depositing this cheque alongside other cheques and cash, select **Undeposited Funds.**

- Print preview and Printing

Select Print or Preview at the bottom of the screen to preview the printed receipt. You can print the receipt by clicking Print from the Print Preview if all is in order.

- Saving for Later

If you do not intend to print this receipt, click the arrow next to Save and submit. Select Save and then close.

- Document of the Deposit

The group deposit must now be recorded in QuickBooks. Under Other on the Plus Sign Menu, select Bank Deposit.

Select the appropriate account, after which insert it under **Add New Deposits.**

How To Setup Advance Payments From Customers

Create a liability that is treated as a liability and holds the retainer or deposit. When you invoice the consumer and obtain payment, this liability will be converted into income.

This is how:

- **Navigate to** Settings > Chart of Accounts**.**
- Select **New**.
- Select **Current Liabilities** from the Account Type drop-down box.
- Select **Trust Accounts - Liabilities** in the Detail Type drop-down menu.
- Provide a username for the account.
- Click **Save**, then close.

Second, a non-inventory or service item must be created for the retainer. Let me guide you on how:

- **Click the** Sales tab**, followed by** Products and Services.
- Select **New.**
- Select **Service** from the Product/Service information screen.
- Enter a name before selecting the **Trust Liability Account** in the Income account.
- Click **Save**, then close.

Create a memo or invoice that will be attached to the newly created invoice. Thus, the invoice will reflect as paid. Follow the below steps:

- Click the +**New button** at the top of the page.
- **Select the** Cash memo **or** Invoice option.
- Choose the Customer from the drop-down menu.
- From the Deposit to the drop-down option, pick the bank account you created for the trust responsibility.
- Select the Retainer or Deposit item you configured in the Product/Service column.
- Enter the amount of the retainer or deposit received.
- Select **Save** and then close.

Manually Adjusting Inventory

- To adjust inventory in QuickBooks Desktop, access the "Adjust Quantity/Value on Hand" box by selecting "Vendors > Inventory Activities > Adjust Quantity > Value on Hand" from the Menu Bar.
- From the "Change Type" drop-down box, choose the type of inventory adjustment to perform. You can modify the "Quantity", "Total Value", or both the "Quantity" and "Total Value" fields.
- The adjustment date must be entered in the "Adjustment Date" box.
- Choose the account affected by the adjustment from the "Adjustment Account" drop-down option.
- Insert an adjustment reference number on the right in the "Reference No." area.
- You can also assign a "Customer: Job" or "Class" to the transaction if necessary.
- Enter the explanation for the inventory adjustment in the "Memo" area at the bottom of the form.
- Then, select the "Item" column on the first available row.
- Choose the first item to be modified from the drop-down menu that appears.
- To create a "Quantity" adjustment, enter either the "New Quantity" or the "Quantity Difference" in the appropriate column.
- If you submit a loss in the "Qty Difference" column, enter a negative amount!
- To adjust "Total Amount," put the new total value in the "New Value" column.

After making inventory adjustments in QuickBooks Desktop, select "Save & Close" to complete the process.

Chapter 9:

Insights and Reports

QuickBooks Online has many customizable reports that can be extremely helpful in making business decisions. Customizable reports will summarize your data and provide reliable, up-to-date information that can be used in your day-to-day operations.

QuickBooks Online offers a wide range of reports depending on your purchased subscription level. As we discussed earlier in this book, the main financial statements include the Balance Sheet, Income Statement, and Statement of Cash Flows. The "Reports" section lets you view, customize, and print these and many more financial statements.

Overview Of Reports And How To Customize

There are several reports that you can run to understand your business better. You can find the reports from the **Dashboard** on the left-hand menu under *Reports*. Most business financials are comprised of three main reports: Balance Sheet, Income Statement (also known as Profit & Loss), and Cash Flow Statement, but QuickBooks Online provides many more statements that can be used for internal purposes.

Reports are divided into three tabs:

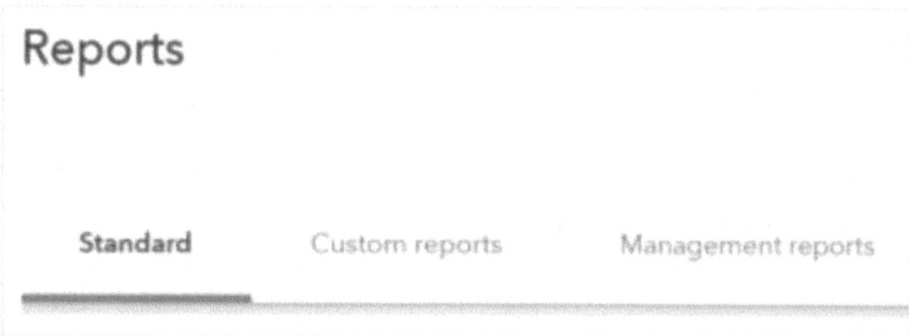

- *Standard* – this tab includes all the reports included in your subscription. These reports can be customized to fit your needs.
- *Custom Reports* – this tab includes all the reports you have created and saved to have the ability to view them in the future.
- *Management Reports* – this tab includes a professional assembly of the basic management financial statements, typically including a Balance Sheet, Profit & Loss Statement, and Statement of Cash Flows.

From the Reports page, you will find the standard reports are broken down into the following categories:

- *Favorites* – this section is customizable by you. You can select the star next to the reports you commonly use to be included in this listing. A few recommended reports to star (besides the common management reports) would include the Accounts receivable aging detail, Sales by Class Summary, and Deposit Detail.

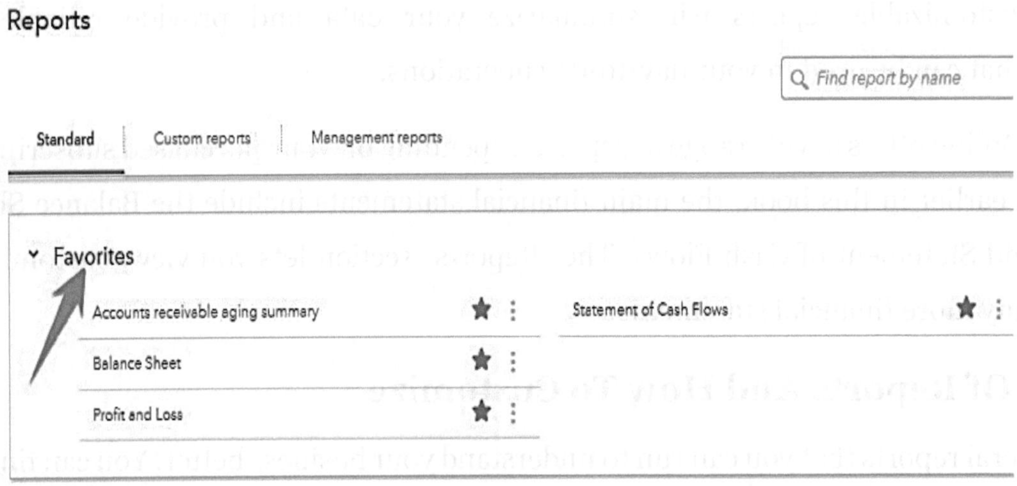

- *Business overview* – includes your key business financials (Balance Sheet & Profit & Loss) in various formats.

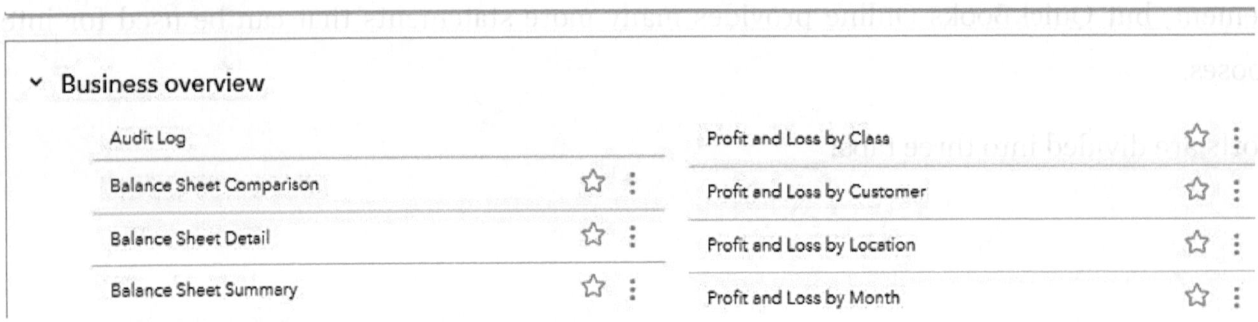

- *Who owes you* – this section includes a variety of reports showing whom you have invoiced, who owes you money, and who has already paid.

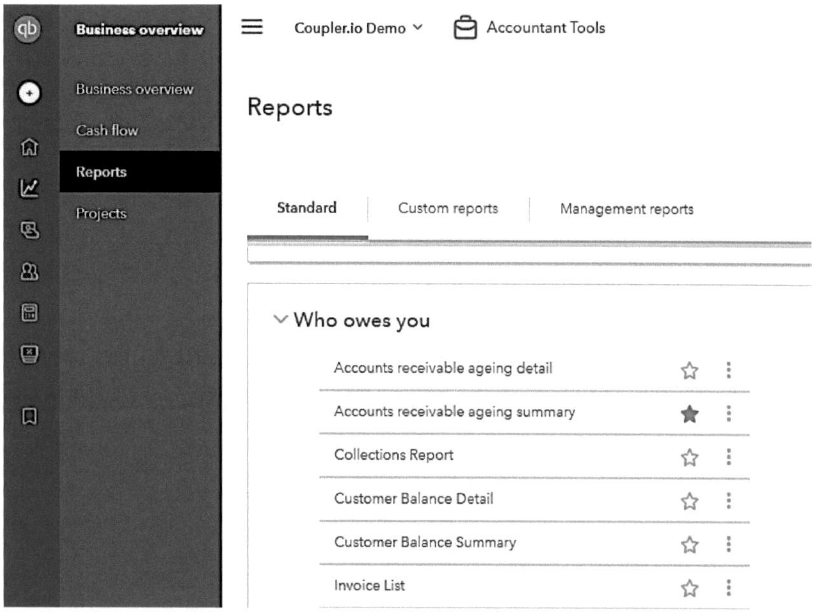

- *Sales and customers* – this section includes all your sales reports and many list reports, including a Customer Contact List and a Product/Service List

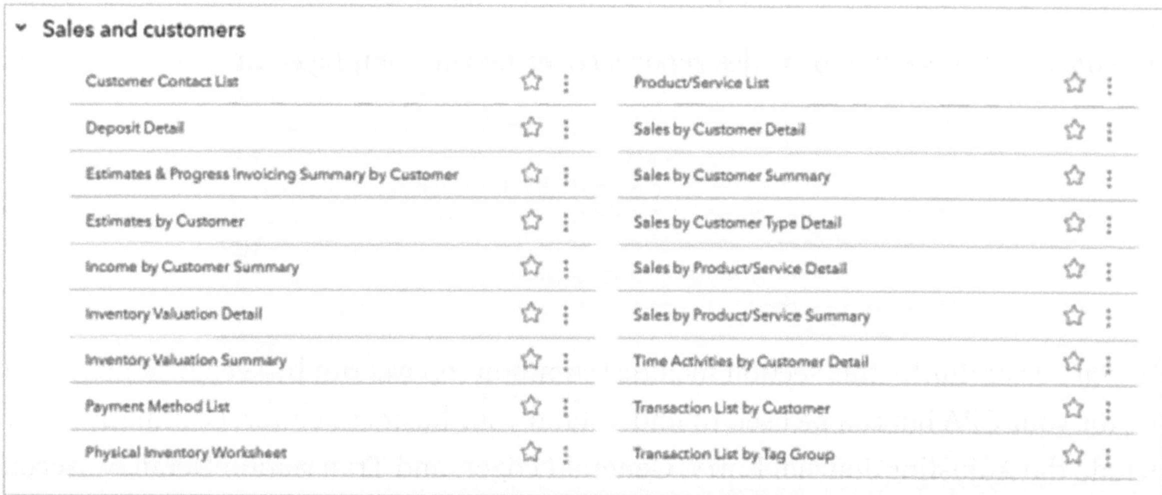

- *What you owe* – includes payable aging reports and additional reports to track to whom you owe money. Additionally, this section has reports for 1099 contractors.

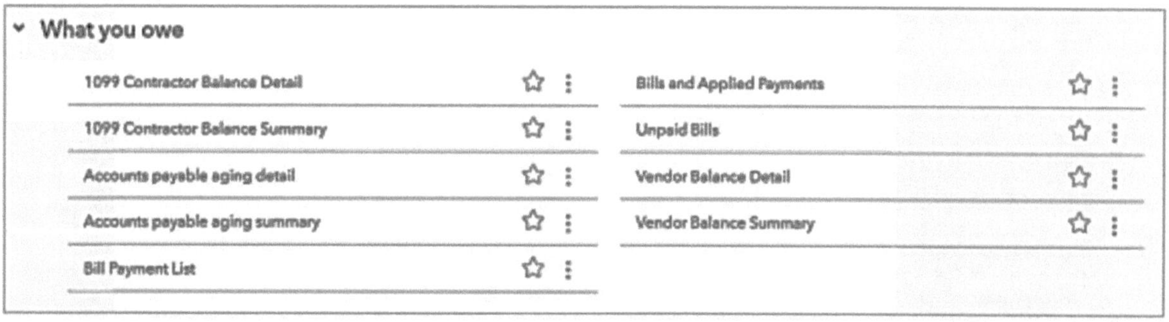

- *Expenses and vendors* – this section includes many reports covering your expenses and vendors. Commonly used reports include the Open Purchase Order List and Transaction List by Vendor.

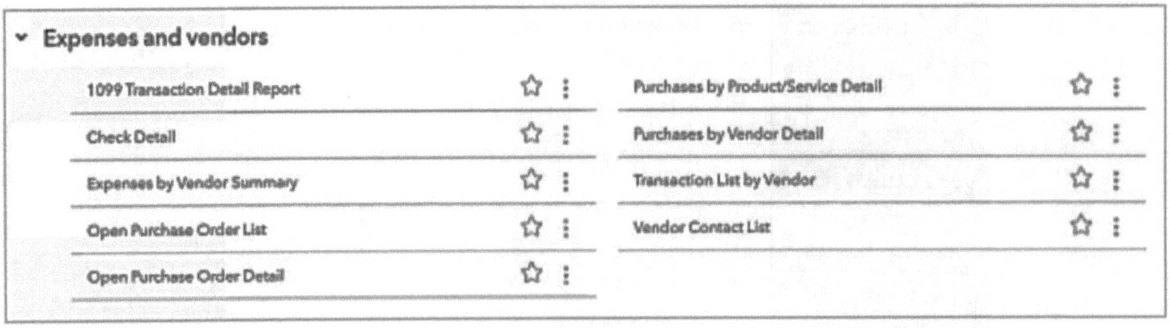

- This section includes your sales tax reports that can be used to review your sales tax liability. This section will only be used by companies selling products or services subject to sales tax.

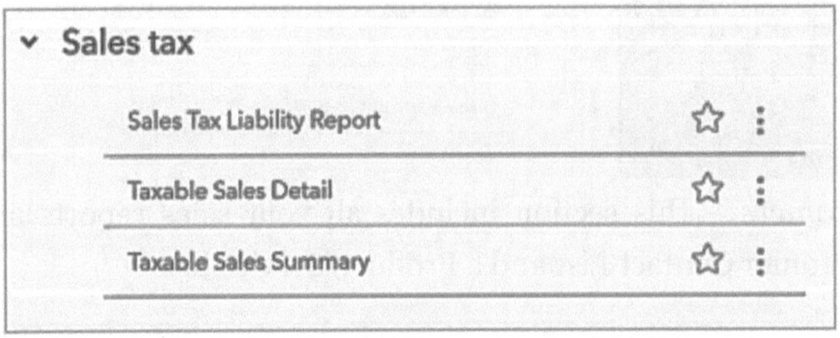

- *Employees* – this section provides reports covering your employee time tracking activity.

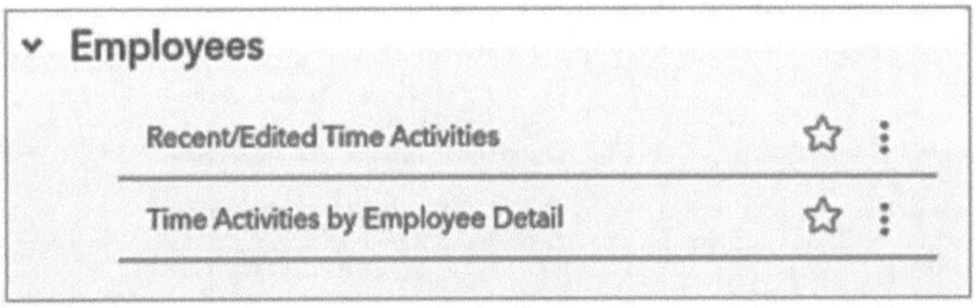

- *For my accountant* – this section includes common reports run by accountants. These are not just for your CPA but can be used to understand your business better. Commonly used reports include the Adjusting Journal Entry, General Ledger, and Transaction Detail by Account.

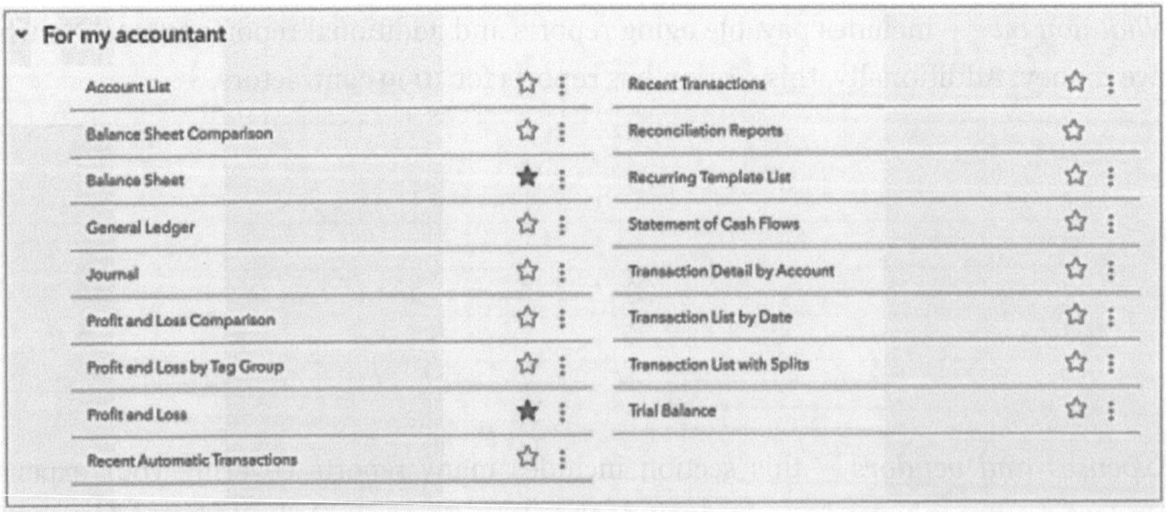

- *Payroll* – this section is for companies running payroll using QuickBooks Online. It includes reports used to review your payroll history, tax liabilities, track employee benefits, and many summary reports.

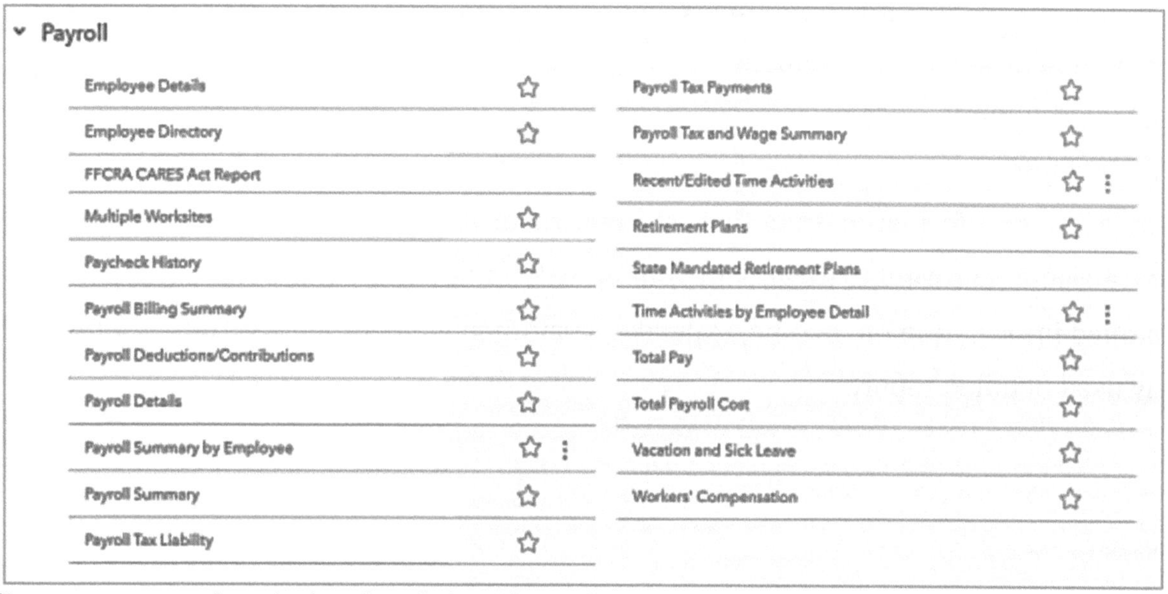

Depending on your subscription level (or if you have a payroll), the subscription will dictate the reports you can see and access. All subscriptions will provide the most basic reports, but the higher the subscription level, and the more reports will become available.

QuickBooks Online uses four main types of reports:

- Summary Reports
- Detail Reports
- List Reports
- Transaction Reports

Summary Reports

These take all your detailed information and compile them into easy-to-understand reports that can be used to compare data. Summary reports are commonly used because they provide a quick snapshot of your data. Here are some of the most frequently used Summary reports:

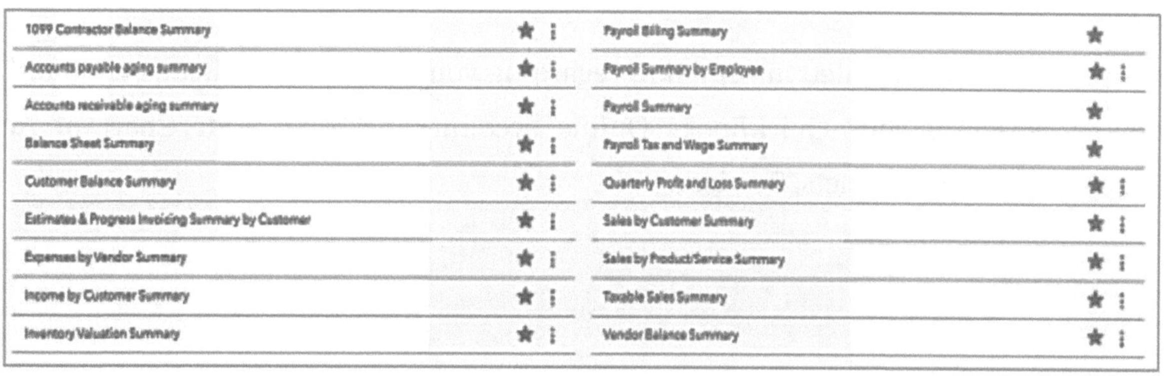

- Balance Sheet Summary
- Profit & Loss Summary
- Sales by Class Summary
- Accounts Receivable Aging Summary
- Accounts Payable Aging Summary
- Payroll Summary

Detailed Reports

These provide more information than the summary reports. These are great when you're looking for a specific transaction or want to document your activity in detail. Detailed reports are used primarily to pull detailed information on income, expenses, customers, and suppliers. Here is a list of the most commonly used detailed reports:

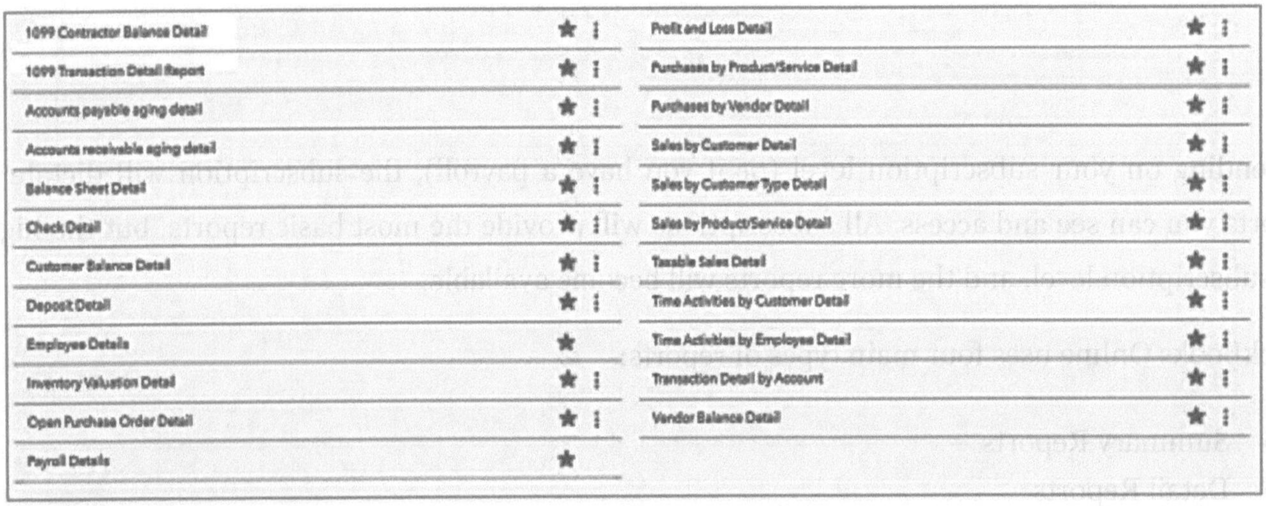

- Balance Sheet Detail
- Profit & Loss Detail
- Deposit Detail
- Accounts Receivable Aging detail
- Customer Balance Detail
- Sales by Customer Detail
- Accounts Payable Aging Detail

List Reports

These are used to provide detailed information regarding your lists in QuickBooks Online. Lists are used in every aspect of your QuickBooks Online account, including your Chart of Accounts, Customers, Vendors, and Products/Services.

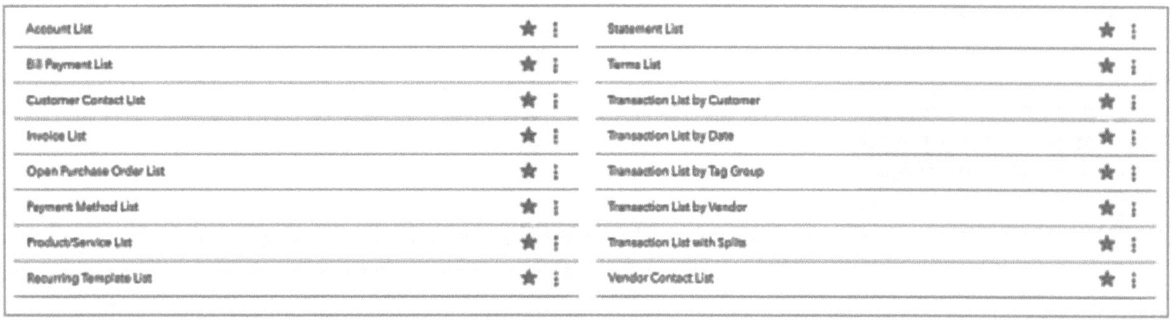

- Account List
- Class List
- Product/Service List
- Vendor Contact List

Transaction Reports

These are the most common type of reports generated in QuickBooks Online. They make up most of the reports and provide key data to make better business decisions. Here are some of the most regularly used transaction reports:

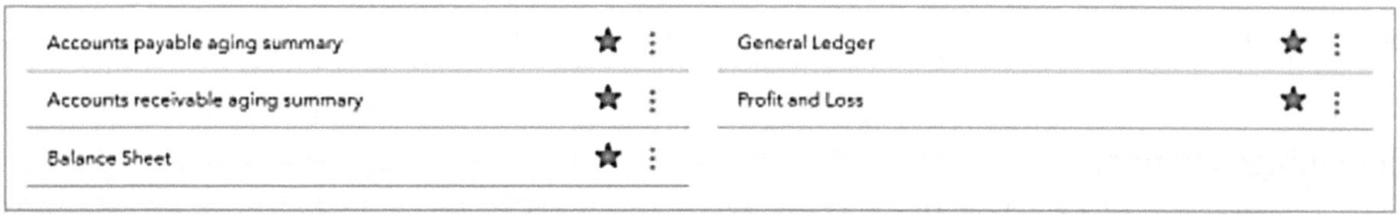

- Balance Sheet
- Profit & Loss
- General Ledger
- Accounts Receivable Aging Summary
- Accounts Payable Aging Summary

Creating And Saving Customized Reports

Customizing reports allows you to change just about everything in a report, including altering the date range, comparing your data to prior periods, changing accounting methods, and customizing the displayed information. To customize a report, select the report you wish to customize, scroll up and select *Customize*.

The custom options are broken down into the following categories:

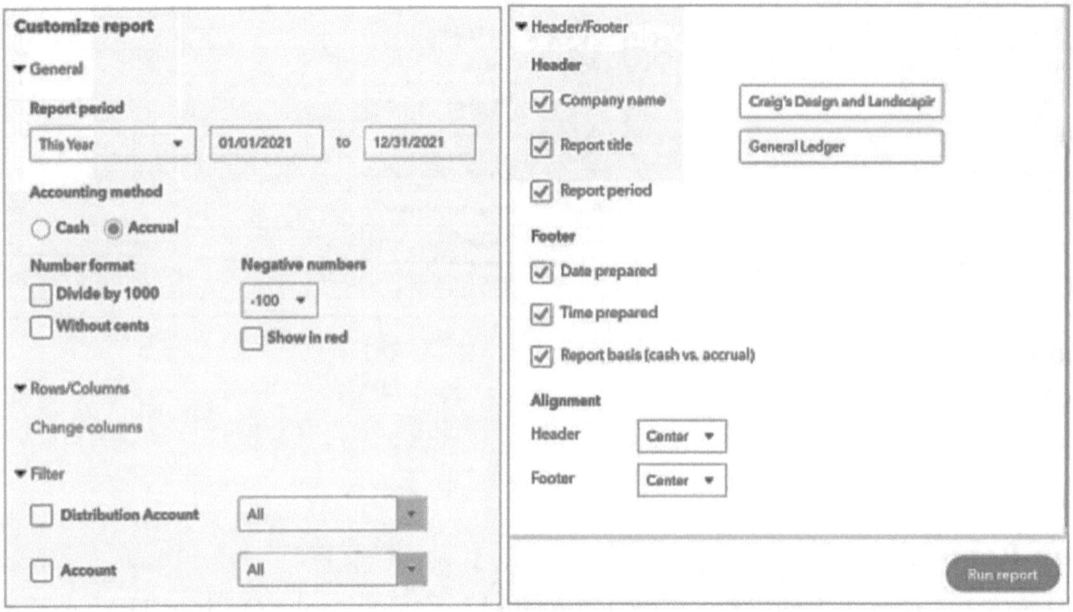

Customize the date range, format, rows, data, and various header and footer options.

- *General* – allows you to select your numbers' reporting period, accounting method, and format.
- *Rows/Columns* – allows you to select the column and comparison column. The comparison column can be either the prior period or the prior year and display the dollar amount or percentage change.
- *Filter* – allows you to select the information you want to be included in your report. You can filter by Customer, Vendor, Class, or Product/Service.
- *Header/Footer* – this allows you to adjust what information is displayed on the header and footer, including the company logo, company name, report title, and report period. The footer includes the date prepared, time prepared, and report basis.

Once you have created the perfect report, it's time to save the report in your "Custom Reports" section. To save a customized report, simply select the green *Save Customization* button. You can rename the report and create groups to categorize your reports. Additionally, you can choose to share your reports with your team or save them for yourself.

Your "Custom Reports" section is easily accessible using the Custom reports tab on the reports home page.

Comparative Reports

Running comparative reports is a great way to evaluate the performance of your business to help make better business decisions. Compare expenses from the prior year, month, week, or another timeframe to determine where your resources are being used. Run comparative reports to evaluate sales growth or trends in your business spending.

Follow these steps to set up and run a comparative report in QuickBooks Online:

1. From the **Dashboard**, select *Reports.*
2. Under the "Business Overview" section, select the *Profit and Loss Comparison* report or *Balance Sheet Comparison.*
3. When viewing the report, scroll up to view the customization options.

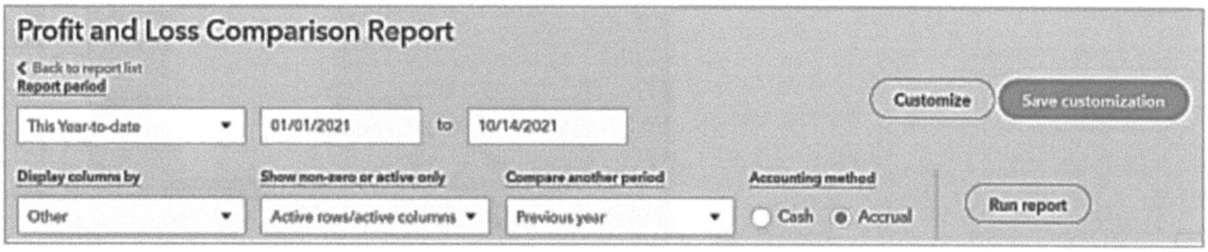

The comparative reports allow you to find variances that may need your attention quickly.

4. Select the Report Period you wish to display.
5. Use the drop-down menu under the "Compare another period" section to select the time period you wish to compare the current period against. You can select to view the difference in an additional column and view the change based on a dollar figure or percentage change.
6. Under the "Accounting Method", select either *Cash or Accrual.*
7. *Select* Run Report.

Setting Up Email Schedules For Reports

Instead of running reports at the end of each period, you can have QuickBooks Online email your custom reports automatically. (Keep in mind that this feature is for custom reports only.) This is a great option if you have multiple owners or investors who want periodic reports. Using this option to send third-party institutions' financials (like a bank or lender) is not recommended, as they should be reviewed and approved before sending.

To set up automatic email reports, follow these steps:

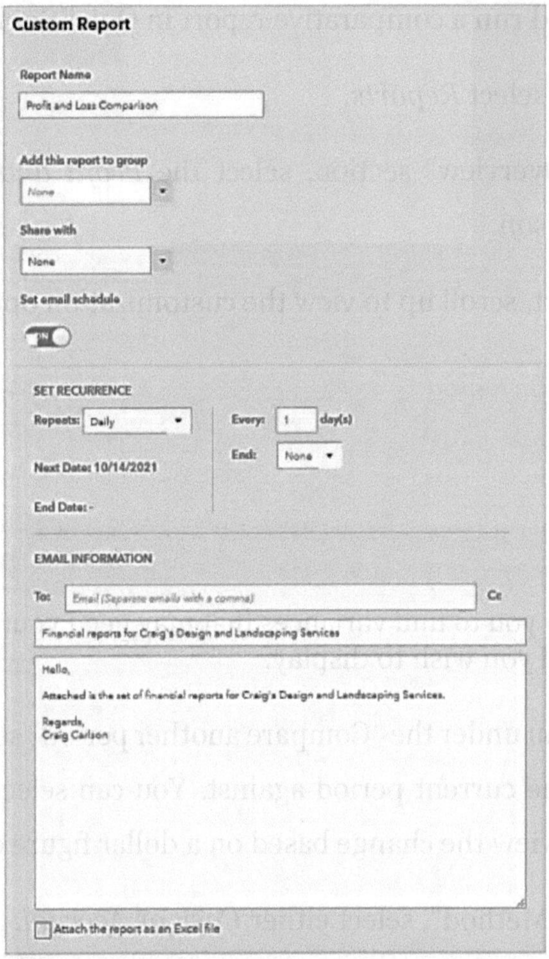

Custom reports allow you to schedule reports to be emailed with a custom message.

1. From the **Dashboard**, select *Reports* from the left column.
2. Select the Custom reports tab.
3. From there, find the report you wish to schedule a reoccurring email.
4. Select *Edit* ✎ from the "Action" column.
5. Under "Set email schedule", use the toggle to select *ON*.
6. Select the recurrence schedule (how often the reports are emailed).
7. Enter the recipient's email address(es).
8. Edit the email subject title and body of the email.
9. Once you are happy with your selections, select *Save and close*.

Audit Log

One of the largest advantages of QuickBooks Online is that it's easily accessible by your employees and accountants. With multiple people in your books, it's important to record what adjustments were made and who made them. The audit log does just that and tracks all the changes in your books and who made each adjustment.

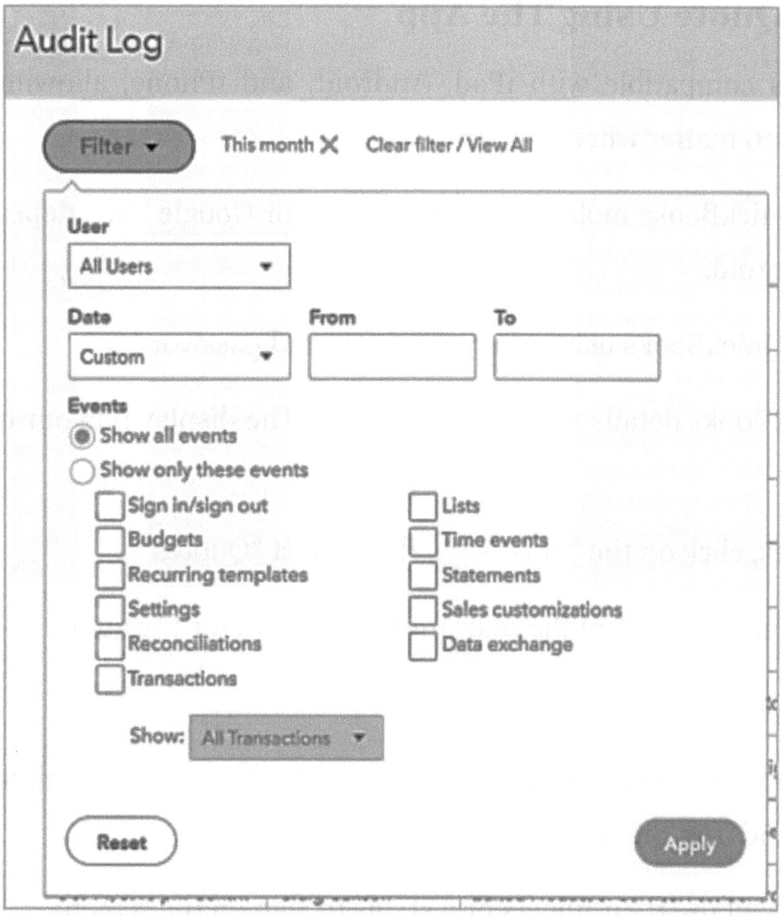

The audit log filter allows you to select the user or date range to narrow your search—track who made adjustments to your books and when.

1. From the **Dashboard**, select the *Settings* icon (⚙).
2. Select *Audit Log* from the "Tools" column.
3. Select the *Filter* to select the user, date, and type of transaction.
4. Select *Apply*.

The Audit log will list all the transactions starting with the most recent. Select the event or history to view more information on a specific transaction.

Chapter 10:

Mobile App

How To Send A Quote Using The App

QuickBooks Online is compatible with iPad, Android, and iPhone, allowing you to access your business information no matter where you are.

First, download the QuickBooks mobile app from iTunes or Google Play, depending on whether you have an iPhone or Android.

1. Log in to your QuickBooks using your username and password.
2. Use your QuickBooks details to sign into the app. The display on your device will be like that on the browser.
3. To create quotes, click on the "Plus" sign, then select "Quotes".
4. Select the customer and input the relevant information for the quote.
5. Email the quotation to the client.
6. The customer accepts the quote by signing on the iPhone or Android phone screen. This is done by clicking on the "Get Signature."
7. The customers will use their fingers or a stylus to sign on the screen.
8. Click "Done" to save the updated quote. The signature captured will be saved as an attachment to the customer quote.

How To Send An Invoice Using The App

1. Open your mobile and go to the "Shortcut" menu.
2. Select "Invoices" and then select "Add New Invoice" near the bottom of the screen
3. In the first field, select the customer or project you are invoicing. If it is a new customer, select "Add" near the bottom of the screen.

4. If you choose an existing customer, you can either assign a new invoice number or leave it blank, and the QuickBooks mobile app will assign a new invoice number in the sequence.
5. Depending on how you configure QuickBooks, today's date will be displayed automatically.
6. Next, select "Add Product or Service". The app will display the list of products and services you are dealing with.
7. Enter the quality and rate you want to appear on your invoices.
8. Enter the applicable tax code for the product.
9. Select "Add" upon completion of product or service update, after which an invoice will display.
10. Select "Save" after inputting all the required details, and you will notice a confirmation that an invoice has been created.

Sending An Invoice Using A Mobile App

1. Select "Send Invoice".
2. QuickBooks will retrieve the customer's email address and display the subject line and email message to customize if desired. You can see the invoice preview that customers will see if they open the email by scrolling down.
3. When you press the send button, you will see the invoice status and date. The status will be updated when the customer views the Invoice. You will also receive payment and deposit updates if you have a payment setup and your bank is linked to a QuickBooks account.

How To Use Receipt Capture

1. Sign in to QuickBooks on your android phone or iPhone using your online user ID and password once you are signed in.
2. Go to "Menu".
3. Tap on "Receipt Capture", and it will automatically open the camera. Take a photo of your receipt or bill.

4. Select "Use this photo" once satisfied with the receipt captured. You will be notified that the receiver has been uploaded to your phone.
5. Go to your QuickBooks Online.

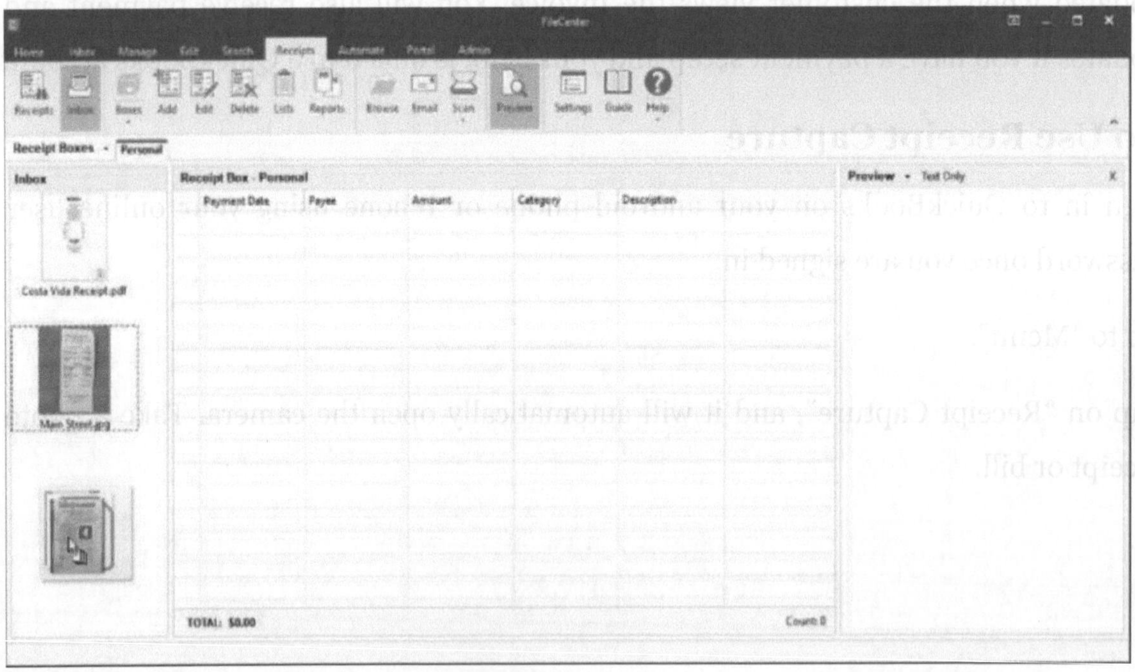

6. Select "Banking" and click on "Receipts".

Here is what you should do if QuickBooks discovers one or more transactions that match your submitted receipt or bill:

1. Click a receipt that will provide a list of the transactions that correspond with it.
2. Select the transaction you wish to associate with the receipt or the bill.

When a receipt or bill does not have a label next to the amount, it simply means QuickBooks cannot locate an existing transaction that matches it. You can only create a new transaction using your receipt or bill as the basis.

1. Select the receipt or bill.
2. Create an expense or bill.

If The Receipt Or Bill Has Missing Information

This indicates that QuickBooks does not extract all necessary information from a receipt or bill and requires additional data or specifications before issuing a bill.

1. Select the receipt or bill to update.
2. Select "Save the Receipt" or bill from the dropdown menu.
3. Create an expense, often known as a bill, for your company.
4. Visit the "Reviewed" page to see a list of all the receipts and invoices you have entered in your books.

Chapter 11:

Bills and Expenses

There are two ways in which to increase the profitability of your business. You can either make more money or spend less on expenses.

Setting Up Vendors

A vendor is a business or individual you pay for a product or service. This could be your paper supplier (think Dunder Mifflen), an IT guy, an office cleaning crew, a utility company, or a marketing firm. Anyone you pay, besides your employees, is a vendor.

Like your customer listing, you can either manually enter vendors or import your full vendor listing to QuickBooks Online. QuickBooks Online has a sample file you can download as a template to format your data into the correct arrangement for upload.

Let's start by looking at how to import your vendor listing from an Excel file. To import your vendor information, you need to have a listing of your vendors' basic contact information, including their names, companies, emails, phone numbers, addresses, and balances for each vendor (if applicable).

Importing A Vendor List To Quickbooks Online

If you were using another accounting software or trusty old Microsoft Excel, you likely already have a listing of your vendors. Uploading your vendor listing to QuickBooks Online is a simple process.

Follow these steps to import your vendors to QuickBooks Online:

1. Select Expenses from the **dashboard** from the left-hand menu, then select *Vendors*.
2. Select the green down arrow next to the *New Vendor* button on the right hand of the "Vendor screen" and select *Import Vendors*.

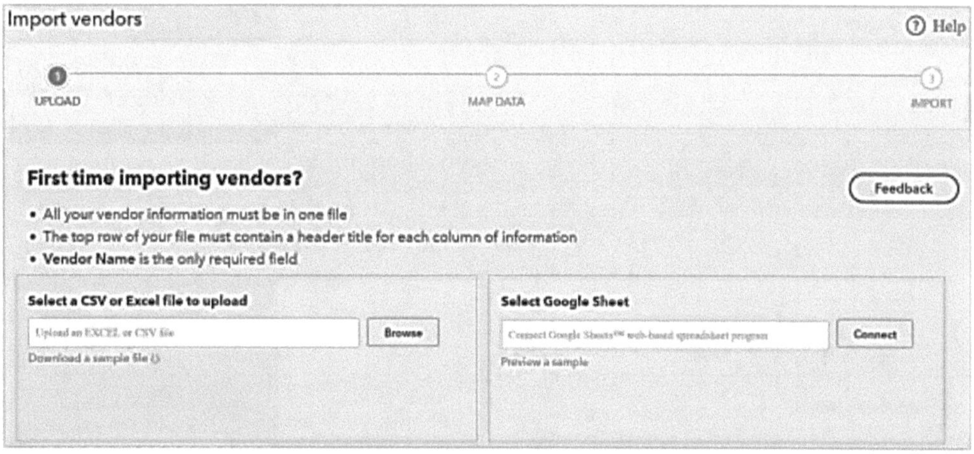

When importing vendors, be sure to add as much info as possible to avoid having to enter data manually.

3. Select the Download a sample file link in the "Select a CSV or Excel file to upload" box.
4. Save a copy of the sample file to your desktop or any other easily accessible folder.
5. Add your data to the Excel sample file, leaving the descriptive header line. Remember to delete the sample data from the file. Once your data is in, save and close the file.
6. Head to the Import Vendors Screen (step 2) and select *Browse* from the "Select a CSV or Excel file to upload" box. Find the file saved on your desktop or folder and select *Open.*
7. Follow the prompts to categorize your vendor data. If you use the sample file, QuickBooks Online will recognize the columns and match the categories properly.
8. Review and import your data.

Once your data is imported to QuickBooks Online, head over to the vendor center and review your listing of vendors, to get to the vendor center from the **Dashboard**, select *Expenses* from the left-hand menu, then select *Vendors.*

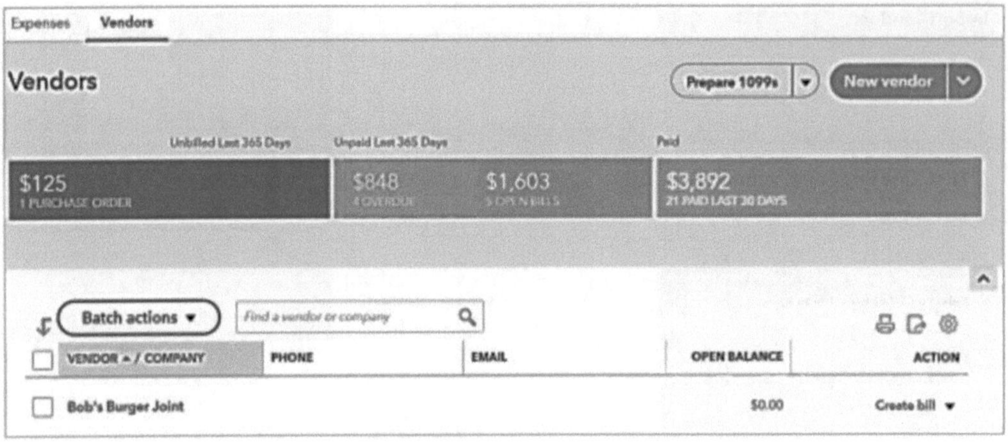

To edit a vendor, select the vendor from the listing and select *Vendor Details*. You can select *Edit* to edit, delete, or update information for a vendor.

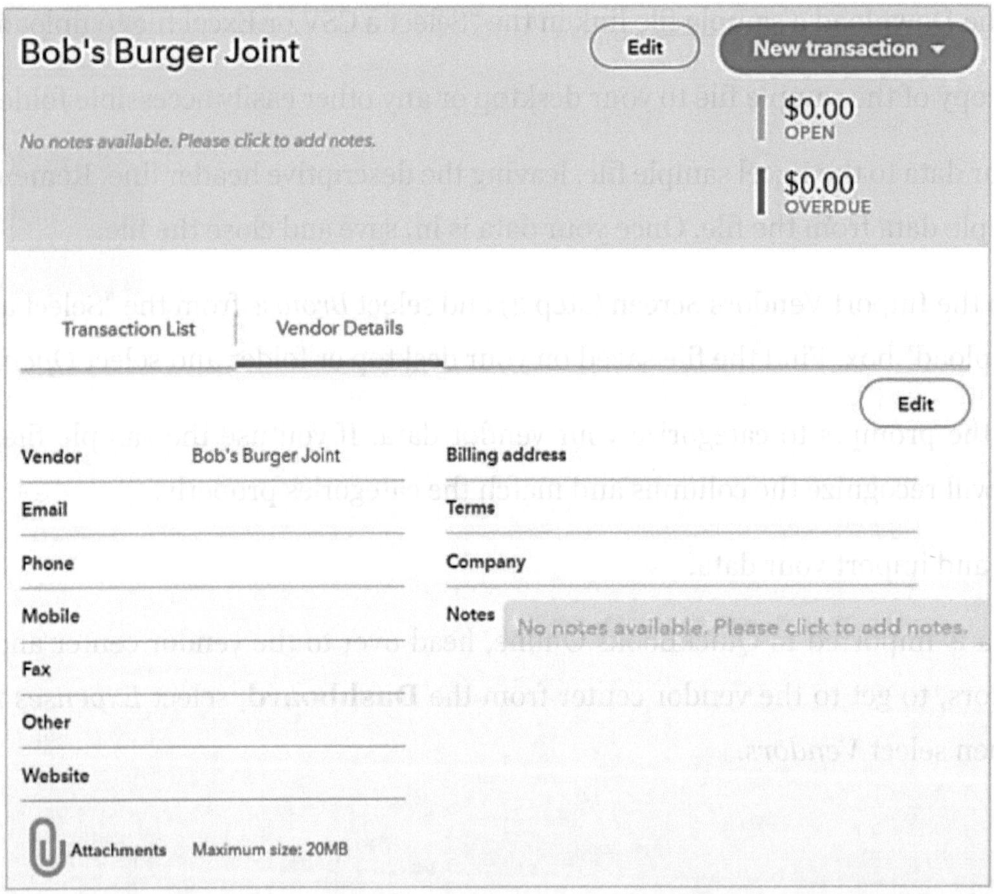

Note that you can also inactivate a vendor from this screen. QuickBooks Online does not allow you to delete vendors or customers from your QuickBooks Online account because it may contain historical information used in prior periods. Making vendors inactive removes them from your current listing without affecting prior data.

Manually Adding A Vendor To Quickbooks Online

Whether you imported your initial listing of vendors or not, you will continue to add vendors as your business grows. There are two easy ways to add new vendors. The first is manually adding the vendor through the "Vendor" section of QuickBooks Online. This process allows you to enter all your vendor's information in a detailed summary page. The second is adding new vendors manually as you enter bills to be paid.

Here's how to input vendors using the manual input screen:

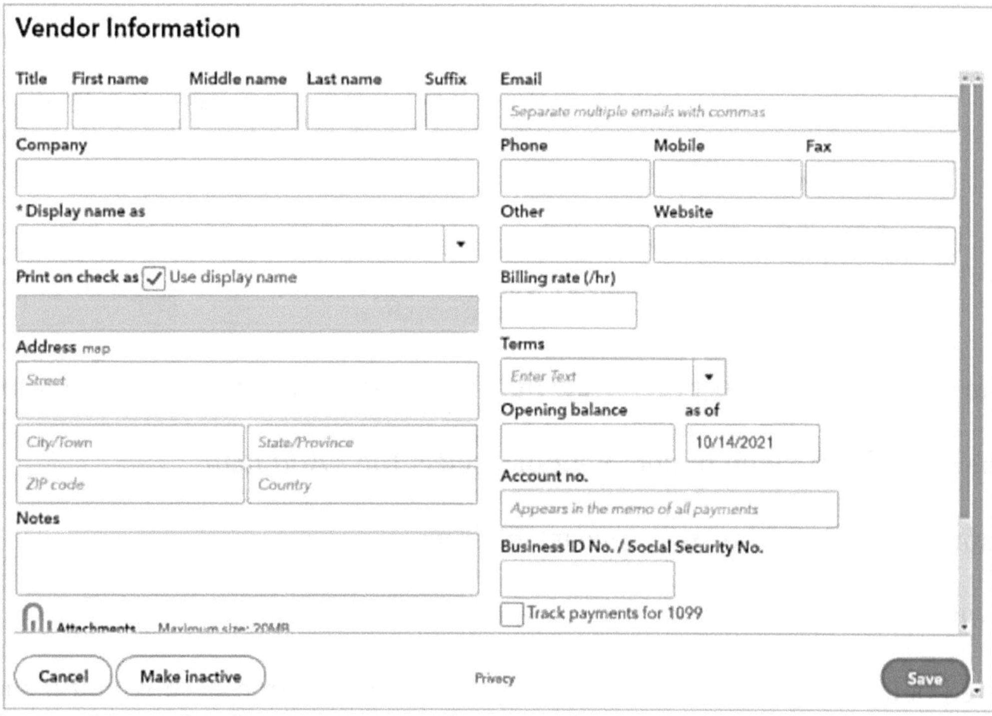

1. From the Dashboard, select Expenses, then Vendors.
2. Select the green New Vendor button.
3. A "Vendor Information" box will appear. Fill it in.
4. Select Save.

To add a new vendor while billing, follow these steps:

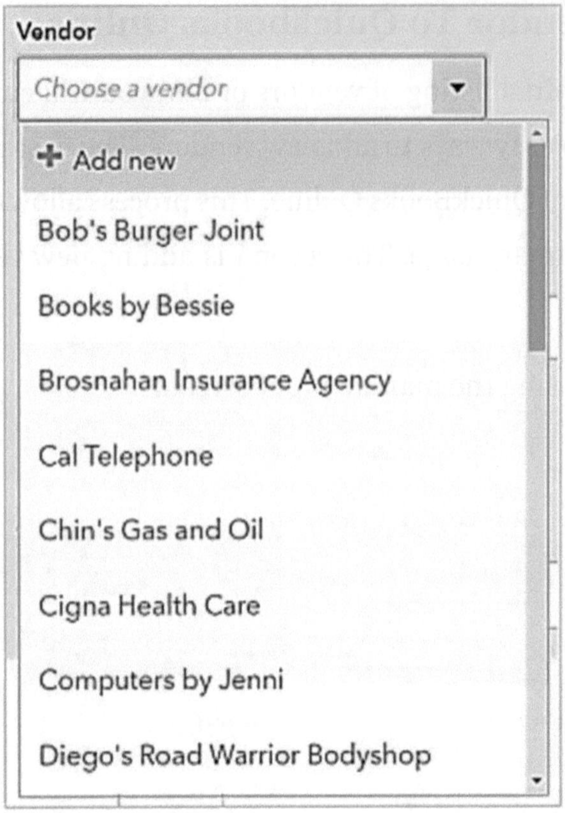

1. From the **Dashboard**, select the *+New* button and select *Bill* under the "Vendors" column.
2. From the drop-down menu under "Vendor", select the *+Add new.*
3. A "Vendor Information" box will appear. Fill it in.
4. Select *Save.*

The only required field when adding a new client is the "Display name as" box, but it's recommended that you add at least the vendor's name, address, phone number, and email address. If you are setting up bills through QuickBooks Online, the software will automatically input the vendor's contact information when creating the bill.

Most of the vendor input fields are self-explanatory, but let's look at some of the more challenging sections:

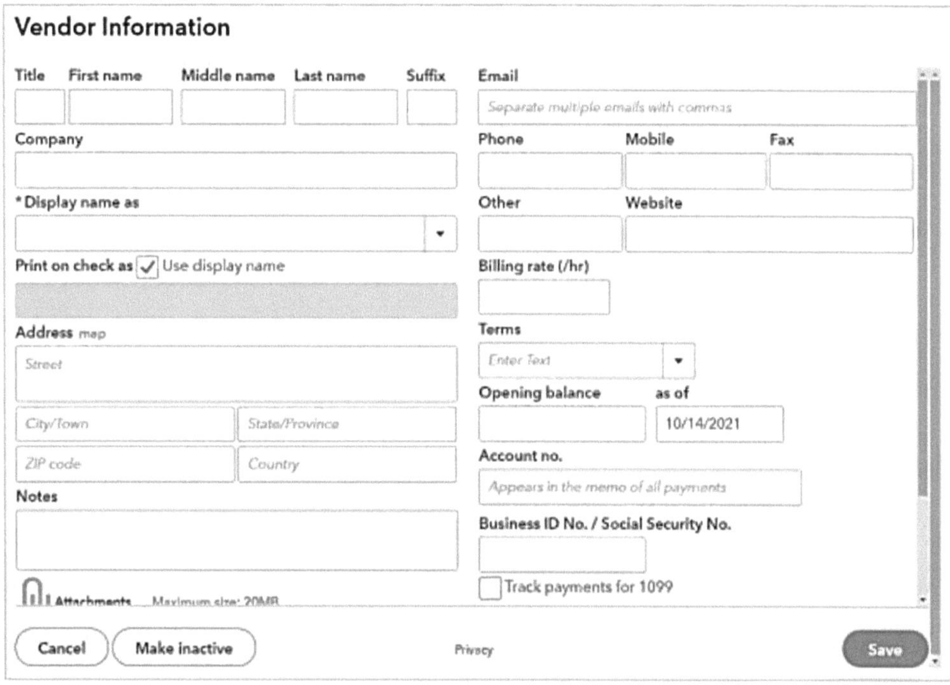

- *Display name as* the required field on the vendor's information input screen. This field will auto-populate if you enter the company name or individual name.
- *Email:* this is the email of the person (or people) receiving your paid bill. When entering this information, you can add multiple recipients by separating the emails with a comma.
- *Billing Rate*: if your vendor charges you by the hour, you can document the rate here.
- *Terms*: here, you can input the agreed-upon terms for this vendor. QuickBooks Online will use these terms to determine when invoices from this vendor should be paid.
- *Opening balance*: if you owed this vendor money when the account was set up, you would enter your balance by the date the vendor was added or the account was created.
- *Account Number*: this would be an account number the vendor assigns to you or your business.
- *Business ID No. / Social Security No.*: If the vendor is a 1099 contractor, you will want to request a copy of their W-9 (Request for Taxpayer Identification Number and Certification) which shows their Employer Identification Number (EIN) or Social Security Number (SSN). If you pay an independent contractor more than $600 during the year, you must issue them a 1099 at the end of the year. Consult with your tax advisor regarding the specific rules for issuing 1099s.
- *Track payments for 1099*: select this box if the vendor is an independent contractor whose income needs to be reported on tax Form 1099.
- *Default Expense Account*: if this particular vendor is always categorized in a certain expense category, select the account here. (Example: Dell Computers may be categorized to the "Computers & Equipment" account.)

As you can see, vendors can be added to QuickBooks Online in several ways. You should take the extra time and complete the input screens with the most information available. It can be difficult to chase down contractors once the year is over to request information needed to file 1099s. The more detailed information added to QuickBooks Online, the easier your reporting will be.

Entering & Paying Bills

Some companies do a great job of tracking revenue but a very poor job tracking expenses. Two ways to increase your bottom line are to increase revenue or decrease expenses. Most companies look to cut expenses when their business hits a downturn. Typically, this is done too late. Knowing where your money is going is just as important as understanding where your revenue comes from.

Entering Bills

Use QuickBooks Online's billing center to record bills you don't want to pay immediately. This creates a short-term payable on your balance sheet. Look at an example, and the journal entry QuickBooks Online will make when you record a bill. Let's assume you are recording your upcoming rent expense for this example.

Here is how QuickBooks Online will book the entry of your rent bill:

	Debit	Credit
Rent	$5,000.00	
Accounts Payable		$5,000.00

QuickBooks Online does a great job producing reports that can help you make business decisions, but you must first enter the information needed to compute the reports. Entering bills into QuickBooks Online allows you to track your upcoming expenses and cash requirements before bills are due. Entering bills into QuickBooks Online allows you to postpone paying vendors until the bill is due, freeing up additional cash for operations. Although entering bills is not required, it is recommended that bills are entered as they are received.

Follow these steps to enter bills into QuickBooks Online:

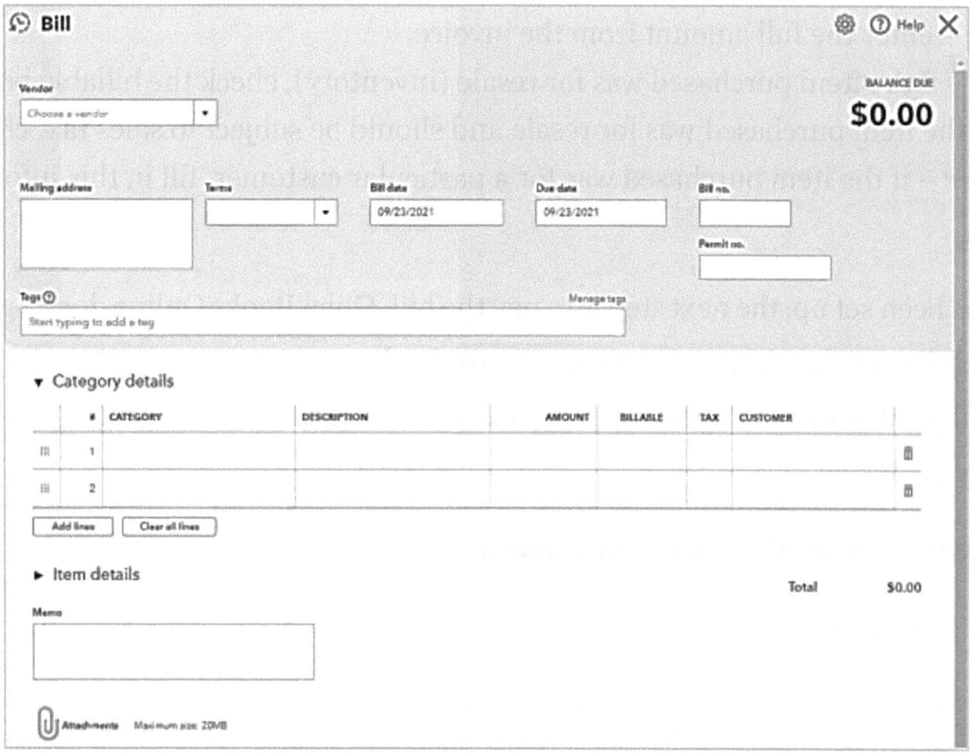

Entering bills allows you to postpone payment until the due date, maximizing your cash on hand.

1. From the **Dashboard**, select the *+New* button and select *Bill* under the "Vendors" column.
2. Complete the required information described below. Remember that your reports and historical documentation will improve the more information is input.
3. Once complete, you can select Save and schedule payment, Save and new, or Save and close.

- *Vendor* – select the vendor you will be paying from your list. To add a new vendor, select *+Add new* from the top of the drop-down menu.
- *Mailing address* – the address will automatically populate based on your vendor data, but you can manually adjust or input this information.
- *Terms* – again, this field will automatically populate based on the vendor data or can be entered manually. This is not a required field if your vendor has not provided you with terms.
- *Bill date* – the date the bill was issued, per the invoice.
- *Due date* – the due date listed on the bill. QuickBooks Online will send you an alert when the invoice is due.
- *Bill no.* – invoice number listed on the invoice.
- *Tags* can be used to generate specific reports for certain groups or events. Tags can be used in your income, expenses, invoices, and bills. Your industry can use tags for certain locations, funnels, product lines, or customer types.
- *Category* – choose the expense category where the bill should be categorized.
- *Description* – enter a brief description of the expense.

- *Amount* – enter the full amount from the invoice.
- *Billable* – if the item purchased was for resale (inventory), check the billable box.
- *Tax* – if the item purchased was for resale and should be subject to sales tax, check this box.
- *Customer* – if the item purchased was for a particular customer, fill in this information here.

Paying Bills

After the bill has been set up, the next step is to pay the bill. QuickBooks Online does a great job letting you know when bills are due, but it's good practice to check your accounts payable weekly to be aware of upcoming bill payments. It's important to pay the bill using the following steps to avoid duplicating the expense in your books.

Here are the steps to pay a bill through QuickBooks Online:

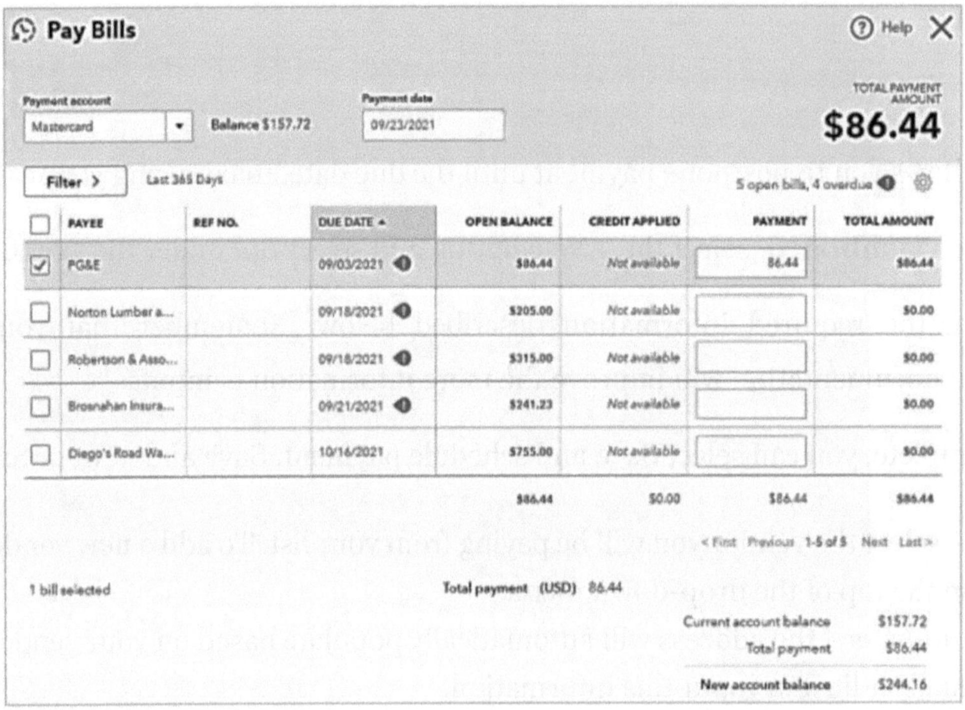

Once the bill has been entered, tracking, and making payments are simple.

1. From the **Dashboard**, select the *+New* button and select *Pay Bills* under the "Vendors" column. Invoices will be listed by the due date. Overdue invoices will be designated with a red exclamation point.

2. Select the payment method and enter the payment date. If you're paying with a check, enter the check number.

3. Select the invoice you wish to pay from the listing of outstanding bills and enter the payment amount. When you select the invoice (using the furthest column on the left), QuickBooks

Online will automatically fill in the full balance in the payment column. If you choose to make a partial payment, enter the amount in this column.

4. Select *Save and print* or *Schedule payments online* to schedule a payment electronically.

Recurring Transactions

Save yourself time by setting up recurring transactions by entering the same invoices each month. Recurring bills can be easily set up using the same bill input screen.

Here are the steps to set up a recurring transaction:

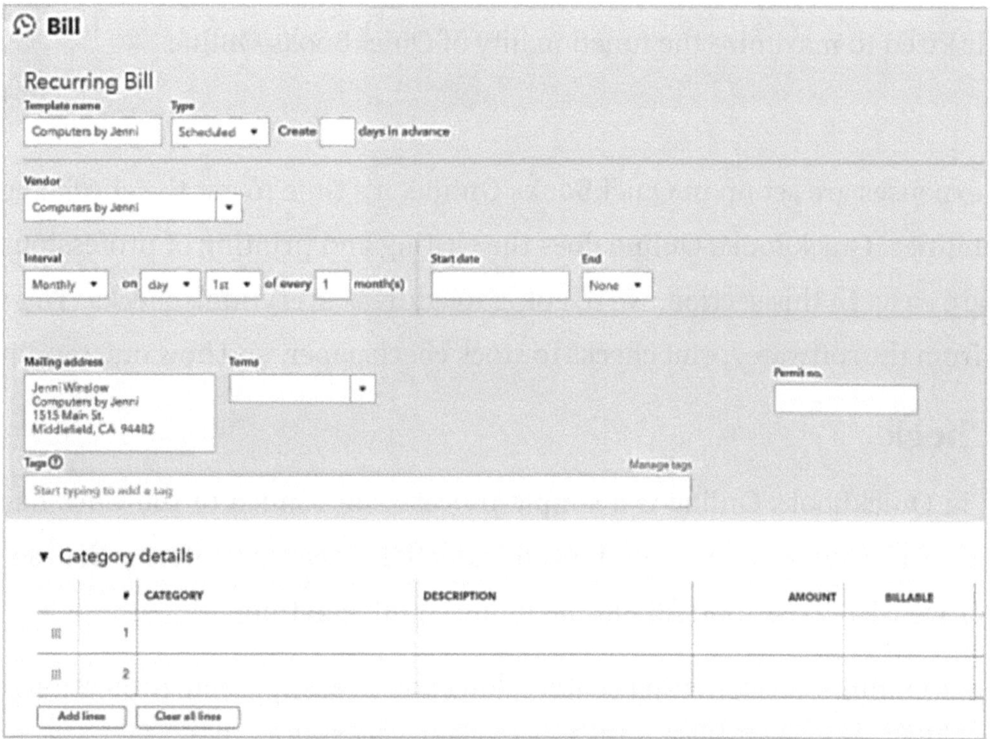

Set up recurring transactions to avoid re-entering the same information each payment cycle. This is perfect for fixed-price expenses like rent or paper shredding.

1. From the **Dashboard**, select the *+New* button and select *Bill* under the "Vendors" column.
2. In the center of the bottom of the screen, select *Make recurring*.
3. Complete the required information described below. Remember that your reports and historical documentation will improve the more information is input.
4. Once complete, you can select the *Save template* button.

The Recurring Bill must also be filled out to the best of your ability to ensure proper documentation and reporting. Here are some important fields to fill out in the input screen.

- *Template Name* – enter the payee's name or an expense description.
- *Type* – using the drop-down menu, select *Scheduled* for bills that have a fixed amount and need to be paid monthly (rent is a good example), *Reminder* for bills that occur each month but have different amounts (utilities are a good example), and *Unscheduled* for bills that are recurring but are not on a schedule (advertising would be a good example).
- *Vendor* – select the payee from the drop-down menu or enter a new vendor using the *+Add new* selection from the top of the listing.
- *Interval* – enter how often the invoice recurs. This could be daily, weekly, monthly, or yearly. You can then select the date on which the bill will be paid.

As you can see, setting up recurring transactions is a great time-saver and yet another great feature that should be utilized to maximize the functionality of QuickBooks Online.

Checks

Now that your expenses are set up in QuickBooks Online, it's time to cut the check and pay off these outstanding liabilities. QuickBooks Online does the writing and printing of professional checks right from the software easy. In this section, we're going to address everything checks. You will learn how to write checks from the software, print checks to stock check paper, and how outstanding void checks.

Writing A Check

Writing checks in QuickBooks Online is a simple process since much of the work has already been completed. We have already set up our vendors and added their contact information, so we can simply select the vendor we wish to pay and fill out the required information.

Using QuickBooks Online's check writing center allows you to easily create professional checks to pay new invoices or bills you have already added to QuickBooks Online. Before we create a check, let's look at an example, and the journal entry QuickBooks Online will make when you create a check.

For this example, let's assume you are writing a check for your rent expense. Here is how QuickBooks Online will book the entry of your rent bill into QuickBooks Online if you have already added the expense as a bill:

	Debit	Credit
Accounts Payable – Rent	$5,000.00	
Checking Account		$5,000.00

As you can see, when recording the payment of a bill in QuickBooks Online, the check will decrease your accounts payable. The payment of a bill is also going to decrease your cash position in your checking account.

Here is the journal entry if the bill has not been added to QuickBooks Online:

	Debit	Credit
Rent Expense	$5,000.00	
Checking Account		$5,000.00

In this scenario, your check payment will increase your expense (rent) and decrease your checking account balance. This is similar to how an expense would be entered into a typical checkbook.

Now that we understand the accounting behind the entry let's look at how to execute the writing of a check in QuickBooks Online.

Here are the steps to write a check in QuickBooks Online:

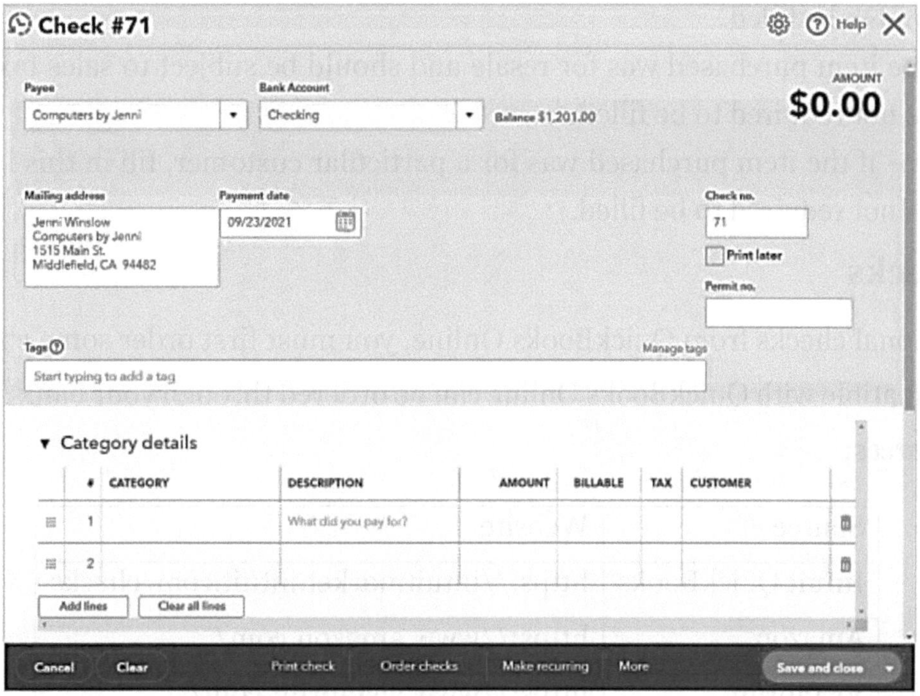

1. From the **Dashboard**, select the *+New* button and select *Check* under the "Vendors" column. The check input screen will appear, displaying the next check number based on your historical entries.

2. Enter the Payee, which will automatically populate the mailing address information. If this is a new vendor, select *+Add new* from the top of the drop-down menu and set up the vendor.

3. Select the Bank Account from which the check will be written.
4. Enter the Payment date and Check number from your checkbook or check stock. You can also select to print a hard check later if you want.
5. Select your Tags only if you are using tags.
6. Fill in the Category details using the explanations below for each cell.

The input screen on a check allows you to enter the required information to complete the check properly. Below are descriptions for each input selection:

- *Category* – choose the expense category where the bill should be categorized.
- *Description* – enter a brief description of the expense.
- *Amount* – enter the amount from the check being written. You can write checks for multiple expenses in one check. For example, a pool supply business may pay an invoice for multiple chemical products in one invoice. They could break out the cost per product on each line.
- *Billable* – if the item purchased was for resale (inventory), check the billable box. This cell is not required to be filled.
- *Tax* – if the item purchased was for resale and should be subject to sales tax, check this box. This cell is not required to be filled.
- *Customer* – if the item purchased was for a particular customer, fill in this information here. This cell is not required to be filled.

Printing Checks

To print professional checks from QuickBooks Online, you must first order some check stock. Check stock that is compatible with QuickBooks Online can be ordered through your bank or online through the following sources:

Source	Website
Intuit QuickBooks	https://intuitmarket.intuit.com/checks
Amazon	https://www.amazon.com/
Vistaprint	https://www.vistaprint.com/

Once you have your checks, it's important to ensure they are formatted properly. Print a sample check on a blank piece of paper to format your checks, so you don't waste your check stock. Hold the printed paper against your check stock to see if it lines up correctly. Checks purchased from Intuit should be formatted correctly, but if you purchase checks from your bank or other online retailers, they may need to be formatted.

To correctly format your checks, follow these steps:

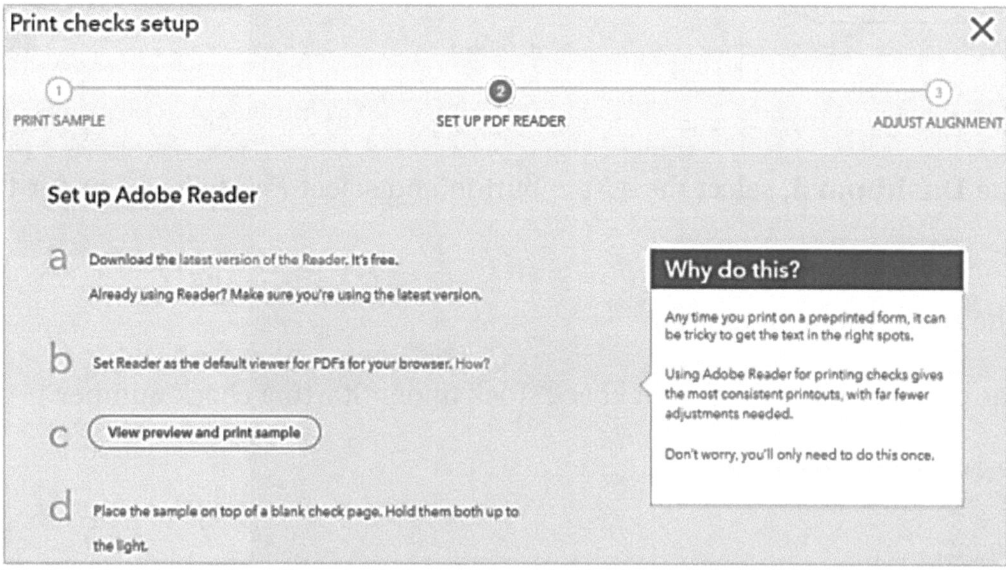

Properly setting up check stock safeguards against printing mistakes and wasting checks.

1. From the **Dashboard**, select the *+New* button and select *Check* under the "Vendors" column.
2. Fill in the appropriate data, including Payee, Bank Account, Category, and Amount.
3. Select *Print check* from the bottom center of the screen.
4. Select *Print setup* from the bottom center of the screen.
5. Follow the steps to print a sample page.
6. Compare the sample page to your check stock.
7. If the placement on the check does not line up, select *No, and continue setup*.
8. Adjust the grid to show where the numbers are displayed on your sample.
9. Select Finish setup.

Once the check is properly formatted, printing the check is a straightforward process.

Here are the steps to print a check in QuickBooks Online:

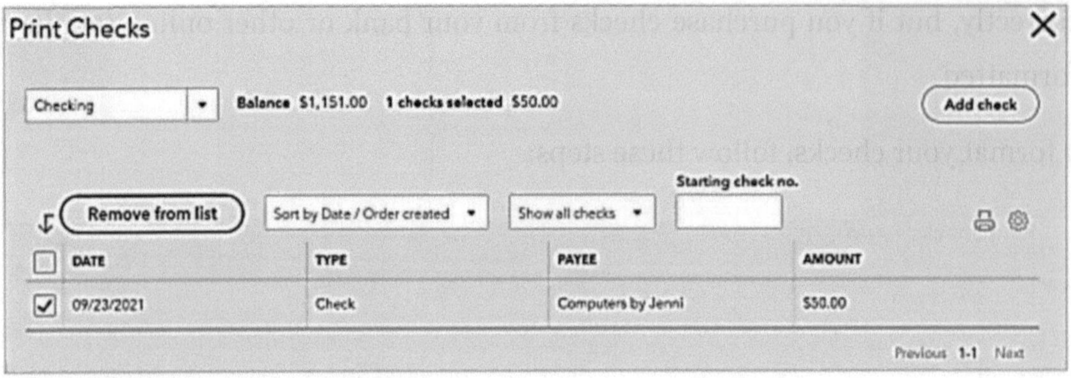

1. From the **Dashboard**, select the *+New* button and select *Print checks* under the "Vendors" column.
2. Select the check you wish to print.
3. Enter the check number from your check stock under Starting check number.
4. Select Preview and Print.
5. Select *Print*.

There you go! Printing checks in QuickBooks Online is a simple process once you get the correct check stock.

Voiding A Check

Everyone is familiar with the practice of writing "VOID" across a check when you make a mistake or need a voided check to set up electronic payments. This indicates that the check is no longer valid and should not be accepted by any bank or vendor. QuickBooks Online uses a similar process to void a check electronically.

Avoid deleting checks, as this also deletes your audit log's transaction history and footprint. You must document a voided check to ensure you don't accidentally reuse a check number and prevent someone from fraudulently generating a check using the same check number.

QuickBooks Online makes it easy to void a check, allowing you to have clean financials with documentation of any missing checks.

Here are the steps to void a check in QuickBooks Online:

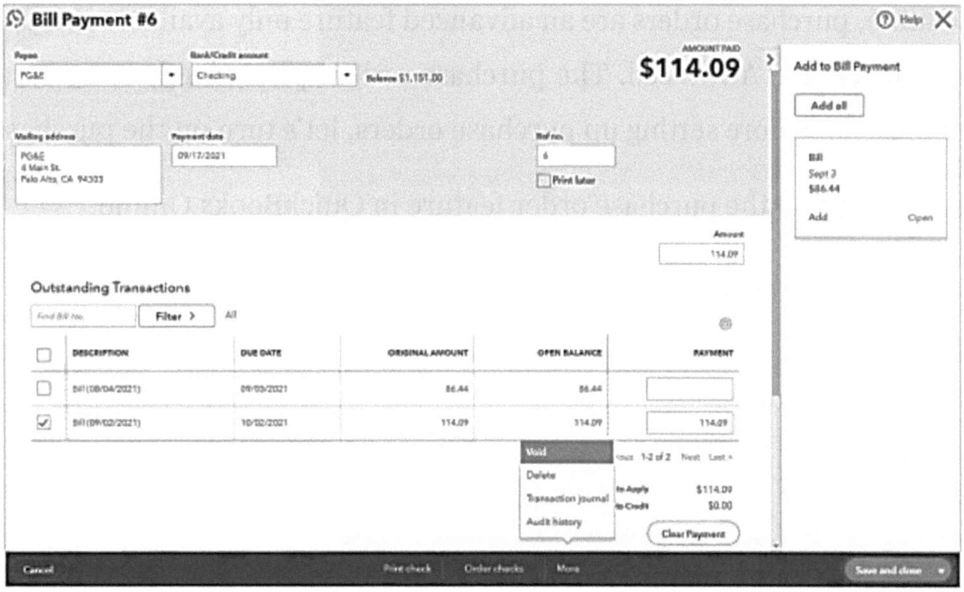

1. From the **Dashboard**, select the *Banking* option from the left-hand toolbar.
2. Select the checking account from which the check needs to be voided.
3. Click the Go to Bank Register link
4. From the bank, register, select the *Find* icon and enter the check number to be voided.
5. Select the check to be voided and click *Edit* .
6. From the bottom center menu, select *More*, then select *Void*.
7. A "confirmation" box will appear; select *Yes*.
8. Select *OK*.

Once the check is voided, any related bills will remain open, and your payable reports will also update. It's always a good idea to confirm that the check was correctly voided by heading to the register and finding the check. The check will be labeled voided in the "Memo" section.

Purchase Orders

A purchase order (PO) is a document from the buyer to the seller requesting inventory or products based on previously agreed upon terms. A PO typically includes the purchaser's account number, tracking number, description of requested products, quantities, and prices.

Purchase orders in QuickBooks Online do not impact your financial statements. Instead, they are just for tracking purposes.

In QuickBooks Online, purchase orders are an advanced feature only available in QuickBooks Online Plus and QuickBooks Online Advanced. The purchase order option needs to be turned on through your account settings. So, before setting up purchase orders, let's turn on the purchase order feature.

Here are the steps to turn on the purchase order feature in QuickBooks Online:

1. Under the *Settings* icon ( ), select *Account and settings* under the "Your Company" column.

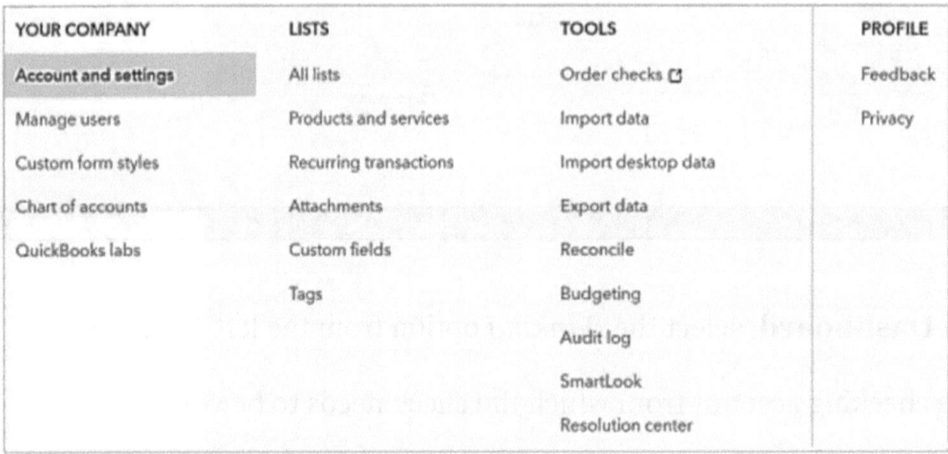

2. Select the Expense tab from the left-hand column.

3. Select Purchase orders.

4. Turn on the *Use Purchase Orders* option.

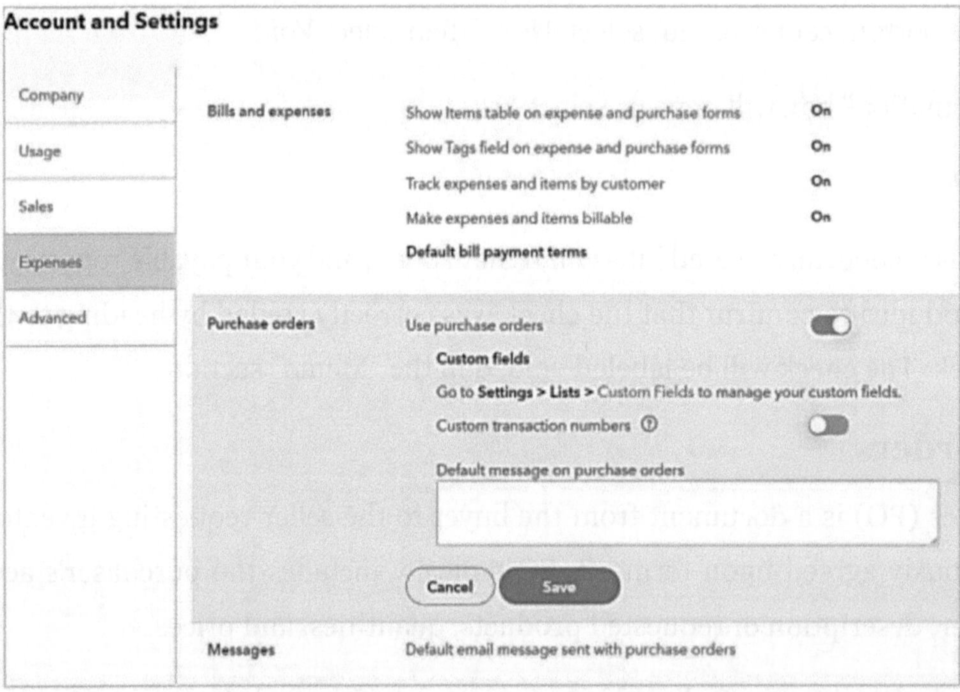

5. You can add custom fields or enter a default message that will also appear on all purchase orders.

6. Click *Save* and *Done.*

Once the purchase order option has been activated in QuickBooks Online, it's time to create your first PO using the Purchase Order Transaction window.

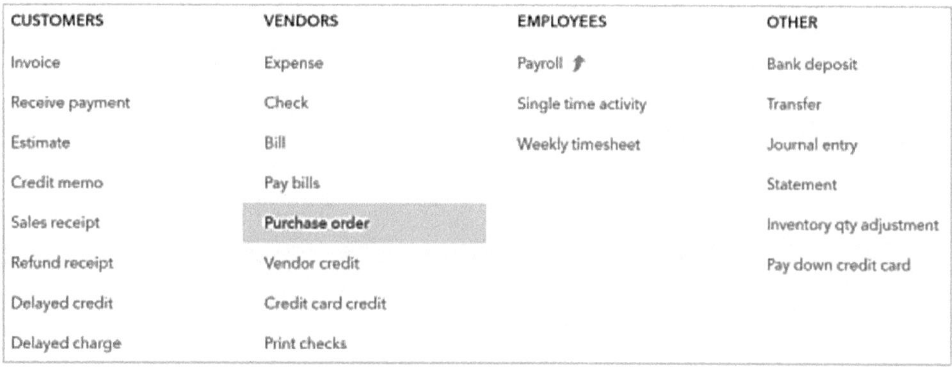

Follow these steps to create a purchase order:

1. From the **Dashboard**, select the *+New* button and select *Purchase Order* under the "Vendors" column.

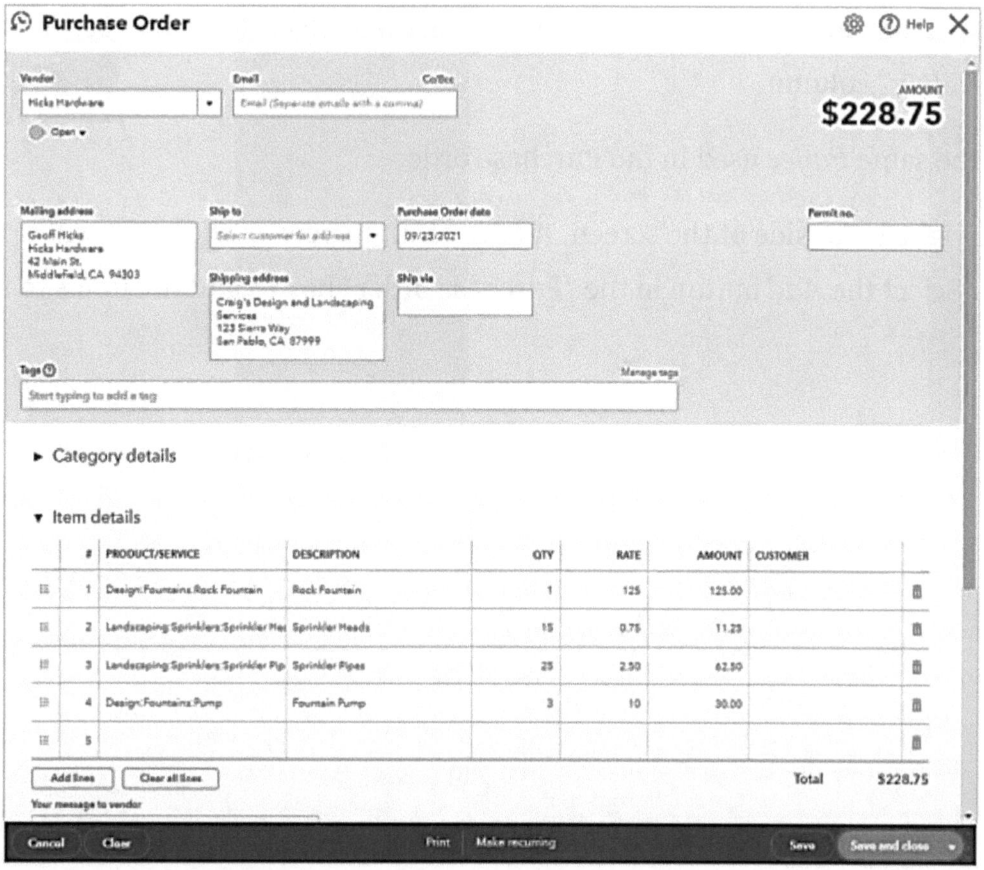

2. Select the Vendor from the drop-down menu. The mailing and email addresses will automatically populate based on the vendor information.

3. Enter the Purchase Order date, Crew #, Ship via, and Sales Rep.

4. Enter Tags, which can be used to generate specific reports for certain groups or events.

5. In the "Item details" section, enter the Product/Service you want to order. The Description will auto-populate. Once you enter the Quantity and Rate, the Amount will also auto-populate.

6. The "Customer" field is optional. If the product or service is for a specific customer, enter this customer here.

7. Once complete, you can select *Save and send* to have the purchase order emailed to the vendor, or you can print the invoice and select *Save and close.*

Once the purchase order has been saved and sent to the vendor, it can be converted to a bill, expense, or check that needs to be paid. So, let's see the steps needed to convert the purchase order.

Follow these steps to convert a purchase order to a bill, expense, or check:

1. From the **Dashboard**, select the *+New* button, then select *Bill, Expense,* or *Check* from under the "Vendors" column.

2. Select the same *Payee* used in the Purchase order.

3. On the right-hand side of the screen, *Add to* (Bill, Expense, or Check) will transition into the screen. Select the *Add* button in the "Purchase order" box to add the items to the transaction.

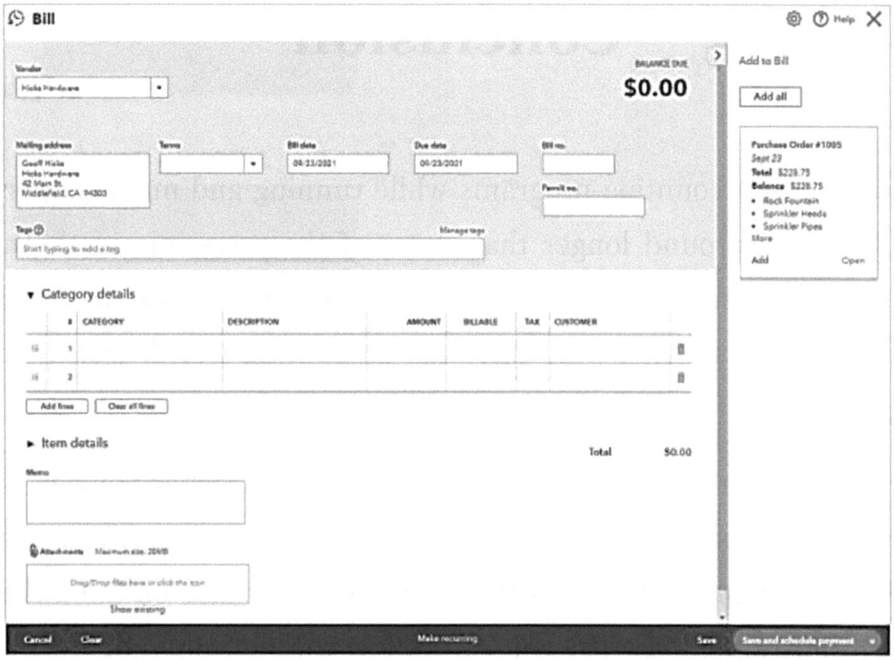

4. Click Save and close.

Remember that purchase orders in QuickBooks Online do not impact your financial statements. Purchase orders are only used for tracking purposes, but once the PO is added to a Bill, Expense, or Check, the item is added to your financial statements.

Conclusion

You will come across many accounting programs while running and managing your business. The QuickBooks suite has been around longer than most of the programs in the market, hence its popularity due to its reputation. Many businesses have used QuickBooks as the backbone of their accounting processes for years. When you enter the accounting world, QuickBooks is one of the accounting packages you might need to learn.

You have a better chance of learning and implementing QuickBooks when you have some background knowledge in accounting or finance. However, this is not always necessary. You will realize from this step-by-step guide that learning QuickBooks is not difficult. We have outlined the important steps and procedures with illustrations so that you can follow through on your own and learn how to manage your accounts.

There is so much to learn from this QuickBooks tutorial that will help you understand how your business operates. You will realise that the point at which you create accounts in QuickBooks matters a lot. At this point, you can create default settings for every customer and vendor account. These settings will cut across all accounts unless you specifically edit them for individual customers and vendors. Why is this important?

QuickBooks monitors and updates all transactions you perform. Therefore, it can keep up with your transactions better than you can. In accounting, no account transactions can be isolated. Every transaction must always affect at least one other account. Each time you make a transaction, QuickBooks updates all the relevant accounts affected by the value of the said transaction. This is why by the end of your accounting period, QuickBooks can populate the necessary financial statements reflecting the financial health status of your business.

When setting up accounts, there are two types of accounting that you can use. Many small and new businesses use cash accounting over accrual accounting. We looked at both of these methods in detail, explaining the content of each one of them and why it is relevant to your business. Many businesses prefer the cash accounting method because it is simple and easy to understand. After all, you are making money, so you record money when you receive or pay for something.

Printed by Libri Plureos GmbH in Hamburg,
Germany